1001
CONTAINER PLANTS

The photos in this book were taken by Bob Aalhuizen, Aat van Wijk and Miep Nijhuis. For their cooperation we wish to thank: Ampi Bouw – 't Harde; Gommer nurseries – Dalen; Nel and Jan Franken – Breda; Jeukens nurseries – Delden; Lavrijssen nurseries – Reusel; Princenbosch nurseries – Gilze; Spek nurseries – Heerde; Exotica nurseries – Herenthout, Belgium; Daubas nurseries – France; Rey nurseries – France; and Wisley Garden – England.

First published in Great Britain 2001

© 2000 Uitgeverij J.H. Gottmer / H.J.W. Becht BV

Printed in Holland for the publishers
B.T. Batsford Ltd.
9 Blenheim Court
Brewery Road
London N7 9NT

A member of the Chrysalis Group plc

Originally published under the title *1001 Kuip- en terrasplanten*
© 2000 Uitgeverij J.H. Gottmer/H.J.W. Becht BV, Postbus 160, 2060 AD Bloemendaal, The Netherlands

ISBN 0 7134 8652 X

1001
CONTAINER PLANTS

Miep Nijhuis

B.T. Batsford Limited

Contents

Introduction

For this book I had to make a selection from the multitude of plants suited for cultivation in pots and containers. You will naturally find – as the title indicates – a large number of container plants. Their assortment has recently been increasing; more and more delicate, typical and interesting plants are now coming to Europe from other parts of the world.

Besides the obvious container plants I have added many plants not known officially as container plants, but well worth cultivating in pots on patios and in gardens. I am thinking of flowerbulbs in the early spring, for instance; it is so nice to admire a pot full of flowering crocuses early in February, or a terracotta container with winter aconites. A bit later in the season there are many annuals which give extra colour to a group of container plants by their exuberant blooming.

You will hardly find any hardy garden plants in this book. Of course you can plant them in a pot, but most of the normal garden plants show to much better advantage in direct soil. Moreover, in a pot they usually only flower for a short period, and on the patio we prefer flowers the whole summer long. However a Hosta, with its long green leaves, will often break up a varicoloured group of plants.

For this book, I have selected plants which, either by their long and exuberant bloom, their leaf form and colour, or their smell, are suitable for cultivation in containers and pots. When combined, they can be an asset to any garden plant arrangement.

Particularities of most of the plants are mentioned under the pictures. I have given special attention to the wintering of the plants.

Most of the photographs have been taken in nurseries. I would like to thank the owners of these nurseries for their hospitality.

A special word of gratitude goes to Nel and Jan Franken, and to Guido van Herck. They assisted me when there were problems concerning the particularities or the naming of plants. It was a privilege to cooperate with these connoisseurs.

And finally, I hope that you, the reader, will read and use this book with as much pleasure as I had compiling it.

Geertruidenberg, March 2000

Miep Nijhuis

Symbols Used

The following symbols are used for the conditions under which the plants flourish best and the lowest temperature they may endure:

☼   full sun
☀   half sun / half shadow
☀   shadow

◊◊◊   plentiful watering
◊◊   normal watering
◊   light watering

❀   The figures next to this symbol indicate in which months to expect a good flowering.

❄   The temperature next to this symbol indicates the lowest temperature (in degrees Celsius) the plant can endure without damage.

n.v.t.   not applicable
zelden   rarely

Important points:

- In order to carry off superfluous water (drainage) it is necessary to have 3 or 4 holes in the container or pot. If there are no holes in the pot, you should pierce them yourself. Put broken pieces of clay flowerpots on the bottom of the pot, with the concave side downwards, or make a layer of expanded clay grains or gravel.
- Plants growing in pots have little room for their roots, and the substrate will be exhausted very soon, so it is necessary to fertilize regularly.
- For plants that flower abundantly and for a long time, weekly nutrition is of particular importance. Even sun-loving plants cannot stand the melting heat of a burning afternoon sun on a tropical summer's day.
- Many plants like to receive plenty of water during blooming, although nearly all plants hate "wet feet". Make sure the roots do not become soaked in times of excessive rain.
- Keeping your plants dry during wintertime does not mean that you should not care for them at all, but the watering must be kept to a minimum. In drizzly winter weather and on short days, it will be more than sufficient to water once a week, presuming your plant is standing in a cool place. When it is freezing it is necessary to give a little extra water, in spite of the advice to "keep the plants rather dry".
- All *Myrtaceae* plants require an acid soil; be wary of root damage when you are repotting. This group of plants must never dry out; if they do, they will lose their foliage, which comes back very slowly.
- Many plants deposit their seeds on the soil (substrate) around the stem – these seeds will then germinate spontaneously. The *Acnictus australis* and *Solanum aviculare* for instance, will produce a lot of young plants around them. You can put the seedlings in small pots, grow them for a few months and maybe give them to "green-fingered" friends.

Owing to an unfortunate error, pictures of *Lavandula dentata* and *Medicago arborea* have appeared twice in this edition.*

☀ ◊◊◊ ❀ 5-10 ❄ 0°C

ABUTILON 'Lemon Bells'

☀ ◊◊◊ ❀ 5-10 ❄ 0°C

ABUTILON *megapotamica*

ABUTILON
MALVACEAE

Propagation: by cuttings.
In the growing season apply a fertilizer weekly;
cut hard back in autumn and keep rather dry and
frost-free; can winter in a dark place; *abutilons* are
obtainable in many colours and every year new
cultivars come onto the market; can be grown as
a shrub or standard; lovely and grateful plants.

☀ ◊◊◊ ❀ 5-10 ❄ 0°C

ABUTILON 'Boule de Neige'

☀ ◊◊◊ ❀ 5-10 ❄ 0°C

ABUTILON 'Mini Orange'

☀ ◊◊◊ ❀ 5-10 ❄ 0°C

ABUTILON *thompsonii*

☀ ◊◊◊ ✽ 5-10   ❄ 0°C

ABUTILON 'Yellow Bells'

☀ ◊◊◊ ✽ 5-10   ❄ 0°C

ABUTILON 'Souvenir de Bonn'

☀ ◊◊◊ ✽ 5-10   ❄ 0°C

ABUTILON hybrid

☀ ◊◊◊ ✽ 5-10   ❄ 0°C

ABUTILON 'Silber Belle'

☀ ◊◊◊ ✽ 5-10   ❄ 0°C

ABUTILON 'Giant Yellow'

☀ ◊◊◊ ✽ 5-10   ❄ 0°C

ABUTILON hybrid

☼ ◊◊ ✿ 6-8 ❄ -5°C

ABELIA *engleriana*
CAPRIFOLIACEAE
Small shrub to 75 cm height; bears panicles of white with yellow and purple flowers from summer to autumn; half-hardy; protect from severe frost.

☼ ◊◊ ✿ 6-8 ❄ -5°C

ABELIA *schumannii*
CAPRIFOLIACEAE
Small shrub to 75 cm height; half-hardy; needs sheltered position; protect from severe frost; attractive to bees.

☼ ◊ ✿ 6-8 ❄ -5°C

ACCA *sellowiana*
MYRTACEAE
Grow in acid soil; never dry out completely; if desired, prune back after flowering; grows on new shoots; don't disturb the root growth; fruit tastes of pineapple; syn. *Feyoa*.

☼ ◊◊◊ ✿ 5-11 ❄ -2°C

ACNICTUS *australis*
SOLANACEAE
Propagation: by cuttings.
Trim branches to encourage bushiness; fertilize weekly; cut back before the winter; grow rather dry and frost-free, if necessary in dark position; syn. *Dunalia australis* and *Iochroma australis*.

☼ ◊◊◊ ✿ 5-11 ❄ -2°C

ACNICTUS *australis alba*
SOLANACEAE
Propagation: by cuttings.
The leaves are larger than the *A. australis*; for cultivation see *A. australis*.

☼ ◊ ✿ 3-12 ❄ 0°C

ADENIUM *multiflorum*
APOCYNACEAE
Succulent perennial for a warm position; very floriferous; keep almost dry during winter and grow frost-free.

☼ ◊ ✿ 3-12 ❄ 0°C

ADENIUM *obesum*
APOCYNACEAE
Succulent perennial; needs a warm position; water sparingly; keep almost dry during winter; grows in desert areas of Arabia and South Africa.

☼ ◊◊ ✿ 5-7 ❄ 5°C

AEONIUM *manriquorum*
CRASSULACEAE
Propagation: divide new rosettes.
Fertilize three times during growing season; grow in well-drained soil; keep dry during winter.

☼ ◊◊◊ ✿ 7-8 ❄ 0°C

AGAPANTHUS *umbellatus*
LILIACEAE
Fertilize weekly; don't repot too often; during winter the plant dies back; can be grown in the dark; in spring give light, warmth, water and fertilizer.

☼   ◊◊◊   ✿ 3-5   ❄ 0°C

ACACIA ***arborea***

☼   ◊◊◊   ✿ 3-5   ❄ 0°C

ACACIA ***balleyana***

ACACIA
LEGUMINOSAE

Propagation: by seed or cuttings in summer. Apply a fertilizer sparely; during flowering season, water freely; some *acacias* produce flowers in winter and early spring as *A. dealbata; A. retinodes* flower during summer; need some pruning in autumn; keep rather dry during winter; *acacias* resist some cold temperatures; lovely flowering shrubs.

☼   ◊◊◊   ✿ 3-5   ❄ 0°C

ACACIA 'Chenille'

☼   ◊◊◊   ✿ 3-5   ❄ 0°C

ACACIA hybrid

☼   ◊◊◊   ✿ 3-5   ❄ 0°C

ACACIA 'Claire de Lune'

☀ ◊◊◊ ❀ 3-5 ❄ 0°C

ACACIA *genistifolia*

☀ ◊◊◊ ❀ 3-5 ❄ 0°C

ACACIA *pendula*

☀ ◊◊◊ ❀ 3-5 ❄ 0°C

ACACIA *peragusta*

☀ ◊◊◊ ❀ 3-5 ❄ 0°C

ACACIA *dealbata*

☀ ◊◊◊ ❀ 3-5 ❄ 0°C

ACACIA *pilligaensis*

☀ ◊◊◊ ❀ 3-5 ❄ 0°C

ACACIA *pravissima*

☀ ◊◊◊ ❀ 3-5   ❄ 0°C

ACACIA *retinodes* 'Lise'

☀ ◊◊◊ ❀ 3-5   ❄ 0°C

ACACIA *saligna*

☀ ◊◊◊ ❀ 3-5   ❄ 0°C

ACACIA 'St. Helena'

☀ ◊◊◊ ❀ 3-5   ❄ 0°C

ACACIA 'Tournaire'

☀ ◊◊◊ ❀ 3-5   ❄ 0°C

ACACIA *trinervis*

☀ ◊◊◊ ❀ 3-5   ❄ 0°C

ACACIA *vestita*

☀   ◊◊◊   ✿ 7-8   ❄ 0°C

AGAPANTHUS ***umbellatus alba***
LILIACEAE
Fertilize weekly; don't repot too often; dies back in winter; keep dry and winter frost-free, if necessary in a dark place; in early spring give light, warmth, water and fertilizer.

☀   ◊◊◊   ✿ 7-8   ❄ 0°C

AGAPANTHUS 'Blue Giant'
LILIACEAE
See *A. umbellatus alba*.

☀   ◊◊◊   ✿ 7-8   ❄ 0°C

AGAPANTHUS 'Blue Moon'
LILIACEAE
See *A. umbellatus alba*.

☀   ◊   ✿ zelden   ❄ 0°C

AGAVE ***americana***
AGAVACEAE
Succulent perennial; decorative plant in combination with flowering conservatory plants; seldom flowers; fertilize sparingly; needs well-drained soil.

☀   ◊   ✿ zelden   ❄ 0°C

AGAVE ***americana marginata aurea***
AGAVACEAE
Succulent conservatory plant; rarely flowers; fertilize sparingly; needs well-drained soil.

☀   ◊◊◊   ✿ 8-10   ❄ 0°C

ALBIZZIA ***julibrissin***
LEGUMINOSAE
Propagation: by seed.
Grows into a splendid tree within a few years; could flower as a young plant grown in a pot; water sparingly during winter; needs a sheltered place.

☀   ◊◊◊   ✿ 8-10   ❄ 0°C

ALBIZZIA ***julibrissin*** 'Rosea'
LEGUMINOSAE
Propagation: by seed.
Grows into a splendid tree within few years; could be flowering as a young plant in a pot; water sparingly during winter; needs a sheltered place.

☀   ◊◊◊   ✿ 4-10   ❄ 5°C

ALLAMANDA ***carthartica***
APOCYNACEAE
Propagation: by cuttings.
Climbing shrub with glossy foliage; very striking and floriferous; fertilize weekly; keep rather dry and frost-free during winter.

☀   ◊◊◊   ✿ 4-10   ❄ 5°C

ALLAMANDA ***carthartica***
'Cherry Sunset'
APOCYNACEAE
Propagation: by cuttings.
Climbing shrub with glossy foliage; striking and floriferous; fertilize weekly; keep rather dry and frost-free in winter.

☼ ◊◊◊ ✿ 4-10 ❄ 5°C

ALLAMANDA *carthartica* 'Chocolate Swirl'
APOCYNACEAE
Propagation: by cuttings.
Splendid when grown as a "pillar" around a wire-form; very floriferous; keep rather dry and frost-free in winter.

☼ ◊◊◊ ✿ 4-10 ❄ 5°C

ALLAMANDA *carthartica hendersonii*
APOCYNACEAE
Propagation: by cuttings.
Flowers are larger than *Allamanda carthartica*; buds are sometimes brown-tinted; the throats have purplish veins; to winter, see above.

☼ ◊◊◊ ✿ 4-10 ❄ 5°C

ALLAMANDA *schottii*
APOCYNACEAE
Propagation: by cuttings.
Smaller than *Allamanda carthartica*; flower looks more trumpet-shaped.

☼ ◊◊◊ ✿ 4-10 ❄ 5°C

ALLAMANDA *violacea*
APOCYNACEAE
Propagation: by cuttings.
Erect semi-climbing shrub; to winter, see above; syn. *A. blanchetii*.

☼ ◊◊ ✿ 5-6 ❄ 5°C

ALOE *arborescens*
ALOEACEAE/LILIACEAE
Propagation: separate offsets.
Needs a mineral soil, mixed with coarse sand or perlite; fertilize sparingly; keep rather dry during winter; syn. *A. perfoliate* var. *arborescens*.

☼ ◊◊ ✿ 5-6 ❄ 5°C

ALOE 'Campert Schweinfurth'
ALOEACEAE/LILIACEAE
Propagation: separate offsets.
Needs a mineral soil, mixed with coarse sand or perlite; fertilize sparingly; keep rather dry in winter.

☼ ◊◊ ✿ 7-9 ❄ 5°C

ALONSOA *warscewiczii*
SCROPHULARIACEAE
Propagation: by seed or cuttings in autumn.
Bushy compact shrub; needs at least 5 °C during winter.

☼ ◊◊◊ ✿ 6-8 ❄ 5°C

ALOYSIA *citrodora*
VERNENACEAE
Propagation: by cuttings.
Twining conservatory plant; lemon-scented foliage; used to make a delicious tea; if wanted, cut back a little in autumn; keep rather dry and frost-free in winter; syn. *Lippia citrodora*.

☼ ◊◊◊ ✿ 6-9 ❄ 0°C

ALPINIA *purpurata*
ZINGIBERACEAE
Propagation: by dividing the rhizomes.
Fertilize weekly; during winter the plant dies back; keep the rhizomes dry and frost-free during winter; early spring re-pot, give light, water and warmth; needs a warm sheltered place; don't keep the plant too wet for long periods.

☀ ◊◊◊ ✿ 4-10 ❄ 5°C

ALYOGYNE *hueglii*
MALVACEAE
Propagation: by cuttings.
Fertilize weekly; take care of well-drained soil; cut back in autumn and keep rather dry and frost-free during winter.

☀ ◊◊◊ ✿ 5-10 ❄ 5°C

ALYSSUM 'Snow Crystals'
CRUCIFERAE
Propagation: by seed.
Grown in pots; fertilize weekly; suitable as groundcover under conservatory plants; sows spontaneously.

☀ ◊◊◊ ✿ 6-9 ❄ 5°C

ANAGALLIS *monelli*
PRIMULACEAE
Propagation: by seed or cuttings.
Splendid annual for baskets; could be wintered, but the results are often disappointing.

☀ ◊◊◊ ✿ 6-9 ❄ 5°C

ANAGALLIS 'Scarlet'
PRIMULACEAE
Propagation: by seed or cuttings.
Splendid annual; suitable for baskets; could survive the winter but the results are often disappointing.

☀ ◊ ✿ 6-7 ❄ 0°C

ANANAS *comosus* 'Victoria'
BROMELIACEAE
The fruits of this pineapple have no hard core; after peeling you can eat the whole fruit.

◐ ◊◊ ✿ 3-4 ❄ -20°C

ANEMONE *blanda*
RANONCULACEAE
Pretty bulbous plant for containers on the terrace in early spring.

◐ ◊◊ ✿ 3-4 ❄ -20°C

ANEMONE *blanda* 'White Splendour'
RANONCULACEAE
Pretty bulbous plant for pots on the terrace in early spring.

◐ ◊◊ ✿ 5-6 ❄ -25°C

ANEMONE *sylvestris*
RANONCULACEAE
Lovely perennial; splendid for pots on the terrace.

◐ ◊ ✿ 4-10 ❄ 0 °C

ANGELONIA *alba*
SCROPHULARIACEAE
Propagation: by cuttings.
Very floriferous conservatory plant with fragrant foliage; keep rather dry in winter; in autumn, cut back a little.

☼ ◊ ✿ 4-10 ❄ 0°C

ANGELONIA **rosea**
SCROPHULARIACEAE
Propagation: by cuttings.
Floriferous twining plant; keep rather dry during winter; cut back a little in autumn; suitable for training along a wire-netting "pillar."

☼ ◊ ✿ 4-10 ❄ 0°C

ANGELONIA **gardneri**
SCROPHULARIACEAE
Propagation: by cuttings.
Very floriferous twining plant; keep rather dry during winter; cut back a little in autumn; suitable for training along a wire-netting pillar.

☼ ◊◊ ✿ 4-6 ❄ 5°C

ANIGOZANTHOS **bicolor**
HAEMODORACEAE
Propagation: by dividing the rhizomes.
Fertilize weekly; let the plant die back before the winter and keep the rhizome dry; replant in spring; give light, water and warmth; 'Kangaroo Paw'.

☼ ◊◊ ✿ 4-6 ❄ 5°C

ANIGOZANTHOS hybrid
HAEMODORACEAE
Propagation: by dividing the rhizomes.
Fertilize weekly; keep rather dry in autumn and winter; replant in spring; give light, water and warmth.

☼ ◊◊ ✿ 4-6 ❄ 5°C

ANIGOZANTHOS **flavidus**
HAEMODORACEAE
See A. bicolor.

☼ ◊◊ ✿ 4-6 ❄ 5°C

ANIGOZANTHUS hybrid
HAEMODORACEAE
See A. bicolor.

☼ ◊◊ ✿ 4-6 ❄ 5°C

ANIGOZANTHUS hybrid
HAEMODORACEAE
See A. bicolor.

☼ ◊◊◊ ✿ 5-10 ❄ 5°C

ANISODONTHEA **elegans**
MALVACEAE
Propagation: by cuttings.
Fertilize weekly; can be pruned during summer; difficult to survive the winter; it is better to start every spring with young plants.

☼ ◊◊◊ ✿ 4-10 ❄ 5°C

ANISODONTHEA **capensis**
MALVACEAE
Propagation: by cuttings.
Give plenty of water to prevent yellow foliage; prune regularly during the growing season; fertilize weekly; difficult to survive the winter; preferable above 5 ºC.

☀ ◌◌◌ ✿ 4-10 ❄ 5°C

ANISODONTHEA **scabrosa**
MALVACEAE
Propagation: by cuttings.
Fertilize weekly; tolerant of heat and drought; needs a well-drained soil; difficult to survive the winter; preferable above 5 °C.

☀ ◌◌◌ ✿ 4-10 ❄ 5°C

ANISODONTHEA **species**
MALVACEAE
Propagation: by cuttings.
Fertilize weekly; tolerant of heat and drought; needs a well-drained soil; difficult to survive the winter; preferable above 5 °C.

☀ ◌◌◌ ✿ 5-7 ❄ 5°C

ANTHEMIS **punctata subsp. cupaniana**
ASTERACEAE/COMPOSITAE
Propagation: by cuttings.
Fertilize regularly; needs well-drained soil; cut hard back in autumn and keep rather dry and frost-free during winter.

☀ ◌◌◌ ✿ 5-10 ❄ 2°C

ANTHIRRINUM **hybrid** lilac
SCROPHULARIACEAE
Propagation: by seed.
To winter the plant, cut hard back in autumn and keep rather dry during winter; sows spontaneously (not invasive); fertilize weekly; splendid for baskets.

☀ ◌◌◌ ✿ 5-10 ❄ 2°C

ANTHIRRINUM hybrid white and yellow
MALVACEAE
Propagation: by seed.
To winter the plant, cut hard back in autumn and keep rather dry during winter; sows spontaneously (not invasive); fertilize weekly; splendid for baskets.

☀ ◌◌ ✿ 6-8 ❄ 5°C

APTENIA **cordifolia**
AIZOACEAE
Propagation: by cuttings.
Pretty, succulent perennial for a warm and sunny position on the terrace; keep rather dry during winter; it is better to take new cuttings; fertilize only once in spring; intolerant of chalk.

☀ ◌◌ ✿ 4-5 ❄ -25°C

ARABIS **flora plena**
CRUCIFERAE
Propagation: by division.
Low-growing perennial; splendid for containers in spring.

☀ ◌◌◌ ✿ 7-9 ❄ 5°C

ARAUJIA **sericofera**
ASCLEPIADACEAE
Propagation: by cuttings.
Fertilize weekly; attractive to moths; the flowers are followed by large green seeds in the next year; for training along a pillar of wire-netting; very striking.

☀ ◌◌ ✿ 5-8 ❄ 5°C

ARBUTUS **unedo**
ERICACEAE
In spring, small white flowers are followed by strawberry-like edible fruits; also named the strawberry tree; winter frost-free and water sparingly.

☀ ◊◊ ✿ 5-8 ❄ 5°C

ARBUTUS **unedo** fruit
ERICACEAE

☀ ◊◊◊ ✿ 5-11 ❄ 4°C

ARCHYRANTHEMUM **frutescens**
COMPOSITAE
Fertilize weekly; cut back in autumn; keep rather dry and frost-free during winter; syn. *Chrysanthemum frutescens*.

☀ ◊◊ ✿ 5-7 ❄ 0°C

ARCTOTHECA **calendula**
ASTERACEAE/COMPOSITAE
Propagation: by seed or division.
Needs a well-drained soil; will survive the winter; it is better to begin in spring with young plants.

☀ ◊ ✿ 5-10 ❄ -1°C

ARISTOLOCHIA **fimbriata**
ARISTOLOCHIACEAE
Climber; especially scented; pretty flower.

☀ ◊ ✿ 4-5 ❄ -25°C

ARMERIA **juniperifolia**
PLUMBAGINACEAE
Propagation: by cuttings or division.
Cushion-forming low-growing perennial; suitable for containers on the terrace.

☀ ◊ ✿ 4-5 ❄ -25°C

ARMERIA **juniperifolia** 'Bevans Variety'
PLUMBAGINASEAE
Propagation: by cuttings or division.
Cushion-forming low-growing perennial; suitable for post on a terrace.

☀ ◊◊ ✿ 6-10 ❄ 5°C

ASARINA **barclayana**
SCROPHULARIACEAE
Propagation: by seed or cuttings.
Climbing plant; suitable for baskets or as a climber; obtainable in various colours; fertilize regularly; difficult to winter; it is better to make cuttings or sow in early spring; syn. *Maurandia*.

☀ ◊◊ ✿ 6-10 ❄ 5°C

ASARINA **barclayana** light variety
SCROPHULARIACEAE
Propagation: by seed or cuttings.
Climbing and trailing perennial; suitable for baskets and as a climber; fertilize weekly; difficult to winter; it is better to make cuttings or to sow early spring; syn. *Maurandia*.

☀ ◊◊ ✿ 5-10 ❄ 0°C

ASARINA **scandens** 'Bride's White'
SCROPHULARIACEAE
Propagation: by seed.
Climbing annual; suitable for baskets; fertilize weekly; syn. *Maurandia*.

☼ ◊◊◊ ✿ 5-8 ❄ -5°C

ASCLEPIAS **currasavica**
ASCLEPIADACEAE
Propagation: by cuttings.
The silky white hairs give it the common name
'Silkweed'; fertilize regularly; cut hard back in
autumn; keep rather dry and frost-free during
winter.

☼ ◊◊◊ ✿ 5-8 ❄ -2°C

ASCLEPIAS **currasavica** 'Silky Gold'
ASCLEPIADACEAE
Propagation: by cuttings.
A bright yellow hybrid from *A. currasavica*; cut
back in autumn and keep rather dry and frost-free
during winter.

☼ ◊◊◊ ✿ 5-8 ❄ -2°C

ASCLEPIAS **fruticosa**
ASCLEPIADACEAE
Propagation: by cuttings.
Flowers are followed by spindle-shaped fruits; fertilize regularly; easy to grow; the fruits are very
striking; cut back in autumn and keep rather dry
and frost-free in winter.

☼ ◊◊◊ ✿ 5-8 ❄ -2°C

ASCLEPIAS **fruticosa** seeds pods
ASCLEPIADACEAE

☼ ◊◊◊ ✿ 5-7 ❄ 0°C

ASCLEPIAS **physocarpus**
ASCLEPIADACEAE
Propagation: by cuttings.
Fertilize weekly; cut back in autumn; keep rather
dry in winter; makes splendid seed pods; syn.
Gomphocarpus physocarpus.

☼ ◊◊◊ ✿ 5-7 ❄ 0°C

ASCLEPIAS **physocarpus** seed pods
ASCLEPIADACEAE

☼ ◊ ✿ 4-5 ❄ 5°C

ASTARTEA **fascicularis**
Conservatory plant; no further details; needs acid
soil.

☼ ◊◊◊ ✿ 4-5 ❄ 5°C

ASYSTASIA **gangetica alba**
ACANTHACEAE
Propagation: by cuttings.
Fertilize weekly; trim long branches; cut back in
autumn and keep rather dry and at 7 °C during
winter; valued for its splendid foliage; syn.
Mackaya gangetica.

☼ ◊◊ ✿ 4-5 ❄ -20°C

AZALEA
ERICACEAE
Needs acid soil; early flowering; lovely on the ter-
race.

☼ ◊◊ ✿ 6-7 ❄ 0°C

AZORINA *vidalii*
CAMPANULACEAE
Evergreen, succulent shrub; leaves grow in rosette; lovely, waxy, long-living flowers; keep rather dry in winter; intolerant of winter wet; not a long-living shrub; easy to grow from seed.

☼ ◊◊ ✿ 5-10 ❄ 0°C

BACOPA 'Snowflake'
SCROPHULARIACEAE
Propagation: cutting.
Also obtainable in rose and lilac; superb for baskets; fertilize weekly; cut back in autumn and keep rather dry in winter, or winter one plant and take cuttings from this plant early spring.

☼ ◊◊◊ ✿ 3-10 ❄ 0°C

BARLERIA *micans*
ACANTHACEAE
Propagation: by cuttings.
Pretty conservatory plant; flowering, with erect spikes; fertilize regularly; keep rather dry and frost-free in winter; replant in spring.

☼ ◊◊ ✿ 5-9 ❄ -5°C

BAUHINIA *corringera*
CAESALPINIACEAE
Propagation: by cuttings.
Lovely conservatory plant; resists some grades of frost.

☼ ◊◊ ✿ 6-10 ❄ -1°C

BAUHINIA *tomentosa*
CAESALPINIACEAE
Propagation: by cuttings.
Lovely conservatory plant with slender, trailing stems; keep rather dry and frost-free during winter.

☼ ◊◊◊ ✿ 7-9 ❄ 0°C

BEAUMONTIA *grandiflora*
APOCYNACEAE
Propagation: by cuttings.
Evergreen vigorous climber with strongly scented flowers; fertilize regularly; cut back after flowering and keep rather dry at 7 °C during winter.

☼ ◊◊◊ ✿ 4-11 ❄ 5°C

BELOPERONE *guttata*
ACANTHACEAE
Propagation: by cuttings.
Place the plant indoors or in a shed during long periods of rainfall; don't cut back before the winter and water sparingly; fertilize regularly during flowering season; shrimp bush.

☼ ◊◊◊ ✿ 4-11 ❄ 5°C

BELOPERONE *guttata alba*
ACANTHACEAE
Propagation: by cutting.
For details see *B. guttata*; the white form from *B. guttata*.

☼ ◊◊◊ ✿ 5-10 ❄ 5°C

BELLIS *perennis*
COMPOSITAE
Propagation: by seed.
Lovely annual; obtainable in many forms and colours.

☀ ◊◊◊ ✿ 3-10 ❄ 5°C

BEGONIA *species*
BEGONIACEAE
Propagation: by cuttings.
Easy to grow; flowers over a long period; fertilize
weekly; upright-growing hybrids need some sup-
port; keep rather dry at 5 °C; if desired, trim in
March.

☀ ◊◊◊ ✿ 3-10 ❄ 5°C

BEGONIA *species*
BEGONIACEAE
See *B. species.*

☀ ◊◊◊ ✿ 3-10 ❄ 5°C

BEGONIA *albo-picta*
BEGONIACEAE
See *B. species.*

☀ ◊◊◊ ✿ 3-10 ❄ 5°C

BEGONIA *fuchsioides* pink
BEGONIACEAE
See *B. species.*

☀ ◊◊◊ ✿ 3-10 ❄ 5°C

BEGONIA *fuchsioides*
BEGONIACEAE
See *B. species.*

☀ ◊◊◊ ✿ 3-10 ❄ 5°C

BEGONIA *maculata*
BEGONIACEAE
See *B. species.*

☀ ◊◊◊ ✿ 3-10 ❄ 5°C

BEGONIA *maculata rosea*
BEGONIACEAE
See *B. species.*

☀ ◊◊◊ ✿ 3-10 ❄ 5°C

BEGONIA *olsoniae*
BEGONIACEAE
See *B. species.*

☀ ◊◊◊ ✿ 3-10 ❄ 5°C

BEGONIA *sutherlandii*
BEGONIACEAE
Propagation: by bulbils.
B. sutherlandii produces bulbils in the leaf axils;
keep dry in peat during winter and replant in
spring; old plants can be thrown away; fertilize
weekly during growing season.

☼   ⬦   ✿ 6-11   ❄ 10°C

BOUGAINVILLEA 'Appleblossom'

☼   ⬦   ✿ 6-11   ❄ 10°C

BOUGAINVILLEA 'California Gold'

BOUGAINVILLEA
NYCTAGINACEAE

Propagation: by cuttings.
Bougainvilleas are not easy to grow; *B. glabra* is the best; it is not difficult to get this plant flowering again.
B. spectabilis needs more attention; grow indoors as long as possible after the winter, until the nights get warmer; they need a sheltered place; before flowering, water sparingly; during flowering water freely, but wait till the plant is rather dry; bring *B. spectabilis* indoors early (September) to adapt; water sparingly during winter; replant in spring and than water freely.

☼   ⬦   ✿ 6-11   ❄ 10°C

BOUGAINVILLEA *glabra*

☼   ⬦   ✿ 6-11   ❄ 10°C

BOUGAINVILLEA 'Dwarf Pink'

☼   ⬦   ✿ 6-11   ❄ 10°C

BOUGAINVILLEA *glabra* light

☀ ◊ ✿ 6-11 ❄ 10°C

BBOUGAINVILLEA *glabra variegata*

☀ ◊ ✿ 6-11 ❄ 10°C

BOUGAINVILLEA *glabra variegata*

☀ ◊ ✿ 6-11 ❄ 10°C

BOUGAINVILLEA 'Italia Pink'

☀ ◊ ✿ 6-11 ❄ 10°C

BOUGAINVILLEA 'Mini Thay'

☀ ◊ ✿ 6-11 ❄ 10°C

BOUGAINVILLEA 'Rosenka'

☀ ◊ ✿ 6-11 ❄ 10°C

BOUGAINVILLEA 'Sakura'

☀ ◊ ✿ 6-11 ❄ 10°C

BOUGAINVILLEA *spectabilis*

☀ ◊ ✿ 6-11 ❄ 10°C

BOUGAINVILLEA hybrid

☀ ◊ ✿ 6-11 ❄ 10°C

BOUGAINVILLEA 'Marie'

☼ ◊ ✿ 6-11 ❄ 10°C

BOUGAINVILLEA 'Australian Gold'

☼ ◊ ✿ 6-11 ❄ 10°C

BOUGAINVILLEA hybrid

☼ ◊ ✿ 6-11 ❄ 10°C

BOUGAINVILLEA hybrid

☼ ◊ ✿ 6-11 ❄ 10°C

BOUGAINVILLEA

☼ ◊ ✿ 6-11 ❄ 10°C

BOUGAINVILLEA *sanderiana*

☼ ◊ ✿ 6-11 ❄ 10°C

BOUGAINVILLEA hybrid

:☼: ◊◊◊ ❀ 4-5 ❄ -25°C

BERGENIA 'Silberlicht'
SAXIFRAGACEAE
Propagation: by division.
Pretty perennial; flowering early spring; when grown in pots, lovely plants for terraces; fertilize regularly.

:☼: ◊◊◊ ❀ 4-5 ❄ -25°C

BERGENIA 'Admiraal'
SAXIFRAGACEAE
Propagation: by division.
Lovely perennial; flowering early spring; a beautiful terraceplant when grown in pots; fertilize regularly.

:☼: ◊◊◊ ❀ 5-11 ❄ 5°C

BIDENS *ferulifolia aurea*
COMPOSITAE
Propagation: by seed or cuttings.
Vigorous annual; suitable for hanging baskets; fertilize weekly during growing season; flowers have a honey-smell; syn. 'Coreopsis'.

:☼: ◊◊ ❀ 6-9 ❄ 5°C

BOUVARDIA *longiflora*
RUBIACEAE
Propagation: by cuttings.
Trumpet-shaped, white, fragrant flowers; needs extra care; fertilize regularly; keep rather dry during winter.

:☼: ◊◊ ❀ 6-9 ❄ 5°C

BOUVARDIA *scabrida*
RUBIACEAE
Propagation: by cuttings.
Slow-growing conservatory plant; fertilize regularly during growing season; keep rather dry in winter; trim untidy stems in spring.

:☼: ◊◊ ❀ 7-9 ❄ 5°C

BOWIEA *volubilis*
HYACINTHACEAE
Propagation: by seed.
Pretty succulent small plant; lovely in baskets because of the whirly growth and green-white flowers; keep the bulbs dry in winter; in spring, replant in mineral soil mixed with coarse sand.

:☼: ◊◊◊ ❀ 5-9 ❄ 5°C

BRACHYSCOME *iberifolia*
COMPOSITAE
Propagation: by cuttings or seed.
Pretty hanger that needs plenty of water; fertilize regularly; obtainable in white, pink and blue.

:☼: ◊◊◊ ❀ 5-9 ❄ 5°C

BRACHYSCOME
COMPOSITAE
Propagation: by seed or cuttings.
Lovely hanger; needs plenty of water; fertilize regularly; leaves are more rough than from *B. iberifolia*; cut back in autumn and keep rather dry in winter; make cuttings in spring.

:☼: ◊◊◊ ❀ 5-9 ❄ 5°C

BRACHYSCOME *iberifolia*
COMPOSITAE
Propagation: by cuttings.
Lovely plant for baskets; needs plenty of water; cut back in autumn and keep rather dry in winter; take cuttings in spring.

☼　◊◊　❀ n.v.t.　❄ -20°C

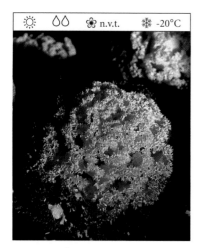

BRASSICA *oleracea*
CRUCIFERAE/BRASSICACEAE
Propagation: by seed.
Lovely annual; gives colour in winter; sow in spring; needs a well-drained soil; best colours are at a temperature under 10 ºC.

☼　◊◊　❀ n.v.t.　❄ -20°C

BRASSICA *oleracea*
CRUCIFERAE/BRASSICACEAE
Propagation: by seed.
Lovely annual; gives colour during winter; sow early spring; needs well-drained soil; best colours are at a temperature under 10 ºC.

☼　◊◊　❀ n.v.t.　❄ -20°C

BRASSICA *oleracea*
CRUCIFERAE/BRASSICACEAE
Propagation: by seed.
Lovely annual; gives colour in winter; sow early spring; needs well-drained soil; best colours are at a temperature under 10 ºC.

☼　◊◊　❀ n.v.t.　❄ -20°C

BRASSICA *oleracea*
CRUCIFERAE/BRASSICACEAE
Propagation: by seed.
Lovely annual; gives colour in winter; sow early spring; needs well-drained soil; best colours are at a temperature under 10 ºC; a flowering cabbage.

☼　◊◊　❀ 3-4　❄ 5°C

BRILLIANTESIS *violaceae*
Little is known about this plant.

☼　◊◊　❀ 5-8　❄ 10°C

BRUNFELSIA *hopeana*
SOLANACEAE
Propagation: by cuttings.
Fertilize regularly; scented flowers; trim in autumn and then keep rather dry and at a minimum of 10 ºC during winter.

☼　◊◊　❀ 6-9　❄ 10°C

BRUNFELSIA *pauciflora*
SOLANACEAE
Propagation: by cuttings.
A compact-growing evergreen shrub; the blue flowers quickly fade to white (this gives the plant its name, 'Yesterday, Today and Tomorrow'); floriferous; fertilize regularly; keep rather dry and at a minimum of 10 ºC in winter.

☼　◊◊　❀ 6-9　❄ 10°C

BRUNFELSIA *pauciflora* 'Macrantha'
SOLANACEAE
Propagation: by cuttings.
Evergreen shrub with flowers larger than *B. pauciflora*, and less fading; flowers well; fertilize regularly; during winter keep dry and at a minimum of 10 ºC.

☼　◊◊　❀ 8-9　❄ -15°C

BUDDLEYA *davidii* 'Pink Delight'
LOGANIACEAE
Propagation: by cuttings.
Hardy shrub with lovely dark pink flowers; in spring, cut hard back to about 30 cm. above ground level.

☼ ◊◊◊ ✿ 6-11 ❄ 0°C

BRUGMANSIA *arborea* 'Engels Glocken'
Dwarf; ca. 1.20 m; floriferous

☼ ◊◊◊ ✿ 6-11 ❄ 0°C

BRUGMANSIA *aurea x arborescens*
Flower held out; fragrant.

BRUGMANSIA
SOLANACEAE

Propagation: by cuttings.
Till some years ago this plant was named *Datura*. Needs plenty of water and weekly fertilizer during growing and flowering season; easy to winter; cut hard back in autumn and keep almost dry in winter, if necessary in dark; the plant loses its foliage and therefore needs little water. In spring, replant and give light, water and fertilizer; the plant absolutely requires an annual replanting to give sufficient growth and flowering.
Brugmansia is a vigorous shrub from 1 to 3 meters high; flowers can be hanging, semi-hanging or held out; they are fragrant, all different and some very strong; a striking shrub; worth growing if you have plenty of space. There is also an annual *Brugmansia* grown from seed.

☼ ◊◊◊ ✿ 6-11 ❄ 0°C

BRUGMANSIA *candida* 'Cinderella'
A new variety with splendid white and salmon-coloured flower; floriferous.

☼ ◊◊◊ ✿ 6-11 ❄ 0°C

BRUGMANSIA *candida* 'Enorm Wit'
Very large trumpet-shaped flower held out.

☼ ◊◊◊ ✿ 6-11 ❄ 0°C

BRUGMANSIA *candida* 'Weisz'
Weeping, firm flower; deliciously scented.

☼ ◊◊◊ ✿ 6-11 ❄ 0°C

BRUGMANSIA 'Gelber Riese'
Huge, firm flower.

☼ ◊◊◊ ✿ 6-11 ❄ 0°C

BRUGMANSIA 'Maya'
A new variety; dwarf ca. 1,25m; pale salmon; variegated foliage.

☼ ◊◊◊ ✿ 6-11 ❄ 0°C

BRUGMANSIA *suaveolens* 'Gold'
Flower held out; free flowering.

☀ ○○○ ❀ 6-11 ❄ 0°C

BRUGMANSIA **suaveolens** 'Goldtraum'
Large flower; free flowering.

☀ ○○○ ❀ 6-11 ❄ 0°C

BRUGMANSIA **suaveolens** 'Silky Rose'
Flower held out; free flowering.

☀ ○○○ ❀ 6-11 ❄ 0°C

BRUGMANSIA **versicolor** 'Jatmer'
Large orange, weeping flower.

☀ ○○○ ❀ 6-11 ❄ 0°C

BRUGMANSIA **versicolor**
White to salmon, weeping flower; huge flower.

☀ ○○○ ❀ 6-11 ❄ 0°C

BRUGMANSIA **versicolor** 'Kew'
White to pink flower, held out.

☀ ○○○ ❀ 6-11 ❄ 0°C

BRUGMANSIA hybrid

☼ ◊◊◊ ✿ 6-11 ❄ 0°C

BRUGMANSIA 'Rosa Glocken'

☼ ◊◊◊ ✿ 6-11 ❄ 0°C

BRUGMANSIA *candida* 'Rosalie'

☼ ◊◊◊ ✿ 6-11 ❄ 0°C

BRUGMANSIA *sanguinea flava*

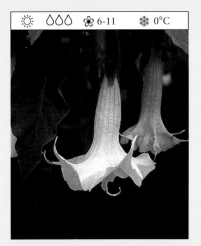

☼ ◊◊◊ ✿ 6-11 ❄ 0°C

BRUGMANSIA *candida plena*

☼ ◊◊◊ ✿ 6-11 ❄ 0°C

BRUGMANSIA *versicolor* hybrid

☼ ◊◊◊ ✿ 6-11 ❄ 0°C

BRUGMANSIA hybrid

☼ ◊◊◊ ✿ 6-11 ❄ 0°C

BRUGMANSIA hybrid

☼ ◊◊◊ ✿ 6-11 ❄ 0°C

BRUGMANSIA 'Pride of Hannover'

☼ ◊◊◊ ✿ 6-11 ❄ 0°C

BRUGMANSIA

☀ ◌◌ ✽ 8-9 ❄ -15°C

BUDDLEYA *davidii* 'Royal Red'
LOGANIACEAE
Prapagation: by cuttings.
Hardy shrub with dark magenta flowers; in spring, cut hard back to about 30 cm. above ground level.

☀ ◌ ✽ 6-7 ❄ 10°C

BULBINE *alcoides*
LILIACEAE/ASPHODELACEAE
Hanging; a succulent tuberous perennial with creeping rhizome; somewhat untidy, but lovely in baskets; keep the rhizome dry during winter and replant in spring; in various colours: yellow, orange and pink.

☀ ◌◌ ✽ 8-11 ❄ -2°C

BULBINE *calocasina*
LILIACEAE/ASPHODELACEAE
Grows in South Africa in rocky places and desert grasslands; needs well-drained soil; keep rather dry in winter.

☀ ◌◌ ✽ 2-4 ❄ -5°C

BUXUS *macrophylla rotundifolia*
BUXACEAE
Propagation: by cuttings.
Very suitable for topiary; needs extra fertilizer after clipping; needs well-drained soil; grown in pots; place out of the sun during a period of frost.

◑ ◌◌ ✽ 2-4 ❄ -15°C

BUXUS *sempervirens*
BUXACEAE
Propagation: by cuttings.
Very suitable for topiary; needs extra fertilizer after clipping; needs well-drained soil; grown in pots; place out of sun during a period of frost.

◑ ◌◌ ✽ 2-4 ❄ -15°C

BUXUS *sempervirens*
BUXACEAE
Propagation: by cuttings.
A good example of how topiary can be applied.

☀ ◌◌ ✽ 8-11 ❄ 2°C

CAESALPINA *gilliesii*
LEGUMINOSAE/CAESALPINIACEAE
Propagation: by cuttings.
Striking, with very long protruding stamens; needs to be fertilized weekly and kept in a warm place; cut back in autumn and keep rather dry in winter; not easy to get flowering plants, but well worth growing.

☀ ◌◌ ✽ 6-9 ❄ -20°C

CALAMINTHA *nepeta subsp. nepeta*
LAMIACEAE
Propagation: by division.
A hardy perennial; splendid for pots; named 'calamint'; fragrant; attractive to bees.

☀ ◌◌◌ ✽ 4-5 ❄ 5°C

CALLISTEMON *citrina*
MYRTACEAE
Propagation: by cuttings.
During flowering season give soft water and fertilize moderately; in winter water sparingly, but do not let the plant dry out completely; prevent leaf drop as it is hard to get new leaves; not all *callistemons* flower well; *C. laevis* is floriferous, *C. citrina* also flowers well, the foliage is lemon scented.

☀ ○○○ ❀ 3-4 ❄ -10°C

CAMELLIA *japonica*

☀ ○○○ ❀ 3-4 ❄ -10°C

CAMELLIA *japonica* 'Adolph Audusson'

CAMELLIA
THEACEAE

Propagation: by cuttings.
Give soft water and fertilize weekly; many *camellias* are half-hardy; give them a sheltered place, protected from wind and sun; at severe frost the foliage evaporates water but is unable to get water from the frozen soil; *camellias* make their buds in autumn and need a cool place in winter; do not let them dry out completely, but too much water is disastrous: keep the golden mean.

☀ ○○○ ❀ 3-4 ❄ -10°C

CAMELLIA *japonica*

☀ ○○○ ❀ 3-4 ❄ -10°C

CAMELLIA *japonica* 'Apollo'

☀ ○○○ ❀ 3-4 ❄ -10°C

CAMELLIA *japonica* 'Benodet'

☀ ◊◊◊ ❀ 3-4 ❄ -10°C

CAMELLIA *japonica* 'Debbie'

☀ ◊◊◊ ❀ 3-4 ❄ -10°C

CAMELLIA *japonica* 'Debutante'

☀ ◊◊◊ ❀ 3-4 ❄ -10°C

CAMELLIA *japonica* 'Hagoroma'

☀ ◊◊◊ ❀ 3-4 ❄ -10°C

CAMELLIA *japonica* 'Italiana'

☀ ◊◊◊ ❀ 3-4 ❄ -10°C

CAMELLIA *japonica* 'Japonia Elegans'

☀ ◊◊◊ ❀ 3-4 ❄ -10°C

CAMELLIA *japonica* 'Jean Claris'

☀ ◊◊◊ ❀ 3-4 ❄ -10°C

CAMELLIA *japonica* 'Marguerita Gouillon'

☀ ◊◊◊ ❀ 3-4 ❄ -10°C

CAMELLIA *japonica* 'Mijakodori'

☀ ◊◊◊ ❀ 3-4 ❄ -10°C

CAMELLIA *japonica* 'Mrs Tingley'

☀ ◊◊◊ ❀ 3-4 ❄ -10°C

CAMELLIA *japonica* 'Snowball'

☀ ◊◊◊ ❀ 3-4 ❄ -10°C

CAMELLIA *sasangua* 'Hiriju'

☀ ◊◊◊ ❀ 3-4 ❄ -10°C

CAMELLIA *japonica* 'Triumphans'

☀️ ◐ ◊◊◊ ❀ 3-4 ❄️ -10°C

CAMELLIA *sasangua* 'Cleopatra'

☀️ ◐ ◊◊◊ ❀ 3-4 ❄️ -10°C

CAMELLIA *sasangua* 'Kanjiro'

☀️ ◐ ◊◊◊ ❀ 3-4 ❄️ -10°C

CAMELLIA *reticulata* 'Dream Girl'

☀️ ◐ ◊◊◊ ❀ 3-4 ❄️ -10°C

CAMELLIA 'Daintiness'

☀️ ◐ ◊◊◊ ❀ 3-4 ❄️ -10°C

☀️ ◐ ◊◊◊ ❀ 3-4 ❄️ -10°C

CAMELLIA 'Sapinic Blanc'

CAMELLIA 'Peach Blossom'

☀ ◊◊◊ ❀ 4-5　❄ 5°C

CALLISTEMON *citrina* seedpods
MYRTACEAE
Propagation: by cuttings.
For details, see above; all *callistemons* are named 'bottlebrush'.

☀ ◊◊◊ ❀ 4-5　❄ 5°C

CALLISTEMON *citrina splendens*
MYRTACEAE
Propagation: by cuttings.
Give soft water and moderate fertilizer during flowering season; the flowers of *C. citrina splendens* are larger than those from *C. citrina* and have white tips on the "bristlehairs."

☀ ◊◊◊ ❀ 7-9　❄ -10°C

CAMPSIS *grandiflora*
BIGNONIACEAE
Propagation: by cuttings.
A vigorous, deciduous climber; frosthardy: -10 °C, but flowering is better in a warm position.

☀ ◊◊◊ ❀ 7-9　❄ -10°C

CAMPSIS *radicans* 'Flamingo'
BIGNONIACEAE
Propagation: by cuttings.
A deciduous climber with large panicles of orange trumpet-shaped flowers; frosthardy.

☀ ◊◊◊ ❀ 7-9　❄ -10°C

CAMPSIS *radicans* 'Flava'
BIGNONIACEAE
Propagation: by cuttings.
Deciduous climber with large yellow panicles of trumpet-shaped flowers; frosthardy.

☀ ◊◊◊ ❀ 5-7　❄ 0°C

CAPPARIS *frondosa*
CAPPARIDACEAE
Propagation: by cuttings.
Keep dry during winter; resists -2 °C; needs a warm place in summer.

☀ ◊◊◊ ❀ 6　❄ 0°C

CAPSICUM *annuum*
SOLANACEAE
Propagation: by seed.
Annual pepper; sow in late winter; needs well-drained soil; give plenty of fertilizer; flowers are insignificant; 8-9 peppers appear (poisonous).

☀ ◊◊◊ ❀ 6　❄ 0°C

CAPSICUM *annuum*
SOLANACEAE
Propagation: by seed.
Annual pepper; sow late in winter; needs a well-drained soil; fruit is poisonous; fertilize weekly.

◐ ◊◊ ❀ 3-4　❄ -20°C

CARDAMINE *quinquefolia*
BRASSICACEAE
Propagation: by division.
Early flowering; after flowering the plant disappears; after spring it comes back into flower.

☀ ◊◊◊ ❀ 7-9 ❄ 0°C

CANNA x 'Oiseau de Feu'

☀ ◊◊◊ ❀ 7-9 ❄ 0°C

CANNA *indica* yellow

CANNA
CANNACEAE

Propagation: by seed or division of the rhizomes. Needs well-drained soil and a warm place; fertilize weekly; dead-head to promote continued flowering; dies back in autumn; store the rhizomes frost-free in sand or peat; replant in spring; divide the rhizomes into short sections, each with a prominent eye; pot these small rhizomes and give them a warm place; soak seed for 24 hours in warm water; sow early; germinates irregularly.

☀ ◊◊◊ ❀ 7-9 ❄ 0°C

CANNA *indica* red

☀ ◊◊◊ ❀ 7-9 ❄ 0°C

CANNA *indica* red-yellow striped

☀ ◊◊◊ ❀ 7-9 ❄ 0°C

CANNA purple

☀ ◌ ❀ 5-7 ❄ 10°C

CARISSA *grandiflora*
APOCYNACEAE
Propagation: by cuttings.
Needs to winter at 10 °C; trim occasionally into shape; large tasty fruits; flowers are very fragrant.

☀ ◌ ❀ 5-7 ❄ 10°C

CARISSA *macrocarpa*
APOCYNACEAE
Propagation: by cuttings.
Fertilize moderately; trim occasionally into shape; winter at 10 °C; after some years, edible fruits appear.

◑ ◌ ❀ 4-10 ❄ 5°C

CARISSA *nana*
APOCYNACEAE
Propagation: by cuttings.
Flowers year-round, with a single flower; keep rather dry in winter, at a minimum of 10 °C.

☀ ◌◌ ❀ 5-8 ❄ -10°C

CARPENTERIA *californica*
HYDRANGEACEAE
Propagation: by cuttings.
Evergreen shrub; frosthardy; loses leaves in severe winters; trim the shrub if it grows too large; needs well-drained soil.

☀ ◌◌◌ ❀ 4-10 ❄ 7°C

CASSIA *artemisioides*
LEGUMINOSAE
Propagation: by cuttings.
Shrub with pinnate leafs and scented flowers; fertilize weekly; very floriferous; cut back in autumn and keep rather dry and frost-free in winter; syn. *Senna artemisioides.*

☀ ◌◌◌ ❀ 6-11 ❄ 5°C

CASSIA *corymbosa*
LEGUMINOSAE
Propagation: by cuttings.
Fertilize weekly; easy to grow; cut hard back in autumn and keep rather dry during winter; syn. *Senna corymbosa.*

☀ ◌◌◌ ❀ 6-11 ❄ 5°C

CASSIA *corymbosa*
LEGUMINOSAE

☀ ◌ ❀ 6-11 ❄ 12°C

CASSIA *didymobotria*
LEGUMINOSAE
Propagation: by cuttings.
Intolerant of too much water; during a long period of rainfall, keep in a dry place (e.g. under a shed); keep rather warm and dry during winter; don't let the plant dry out; not easy, but very striking.

☀ ◌◌◌ ❀ 6-11 ❄ 2°C

CASSIA *floribunda*
LEGUMINOSAE
Propagation: by cuttings.
Fertilize regularly; the growth is more compact than *C. corymbosa*; very floriferous; cut hard back in autumn; keep rather dry at 5 °C during winter; can be placed in a dark position; syn. *Senna floribunda.*

☀ ◊◊◊ ✿ 6-11 ❄ 2°C

CASSIA *floribunda*
LEGUMINOSAE
Flowering shrub.

☀ ◊◊◊ ✿ 4-7 ❄ 2°C

CEANOTHUS *thyrsiflorus var. repens*
OLEACEAE
Propagation: by cuttings.
Fertilize weekly; easy to grow; cut back after flowering; keep rather dry and frost-free during winter.

☀ ◊ ✿ 6-11 ❄ 5°C

CELOSIA *argentea*
AMARANTHACEAE
Propagation: by seed.
Annual; sow early spring; needs well-drained soil; water carefully: not too much, not too little.

☀ ◊ ✿ 6-11 ❄ 5°C

CELOSIA *argentea pyramidalis*
AMARANTHACEAE
Propagation: by seed or cuttings.
Annual; sow in autumn or early spring; needs well-drained soil; water carefully.

◐ ◊◊ ✿ 7-9 ❄ 10°C

CENTHRATERUM *camphorum*
Propagation: by cuttings.
Cut back after flowering; keep rather dry and warm (10 ºC) during winter; rare.

☀ ◊◊◊ ✿ 7-10 ❄ 7°C

CENTRADENIA
MELASTOMATACEAE
Propagation: by cuttings.
Trailing perennial; does not flower before its second year; fertilize weekly; cut back in autumn and keep rather dry at 7 ºC in winter.

◐ ◊◊ ✿ n.v.t. ❄ -20°C

**CEPHALOTAXUS *harringtoniana*
'Fastigiata'**
CEPHALOTAXACEAE
Propagation: by seed or cuttings.
Needs a cool place and well-drained soil; lovely conifer.

☀ ◊◊◊ ✿ 7-8 ❄ -5°C

CERATOSTIGMA *plumbaginoides*
PLUMBAGINACEAE
Propagation: by cuttings.
Lovely colours in autumn; in sheltered places, frosthardy; cut back in autumn and keep rather dry in winter (preferably indoors).

☀ ◊◊◊ ✿ 4-11 ❄ 2°C

CESTRUM *aurantiacum*
SOLANACEAE
Propagation: by cuttings.
Vigorous shrub; fertilize weekly; lightly fragrant at night; white berries; cut hard back in autumn and keep rather dry in winter, if necessary in the dark.

☀ ◊◊◊ ✿ 4-11 ❄ 2°C

CESTRUM hybrid apricot coloured
SOLANACEAE
Propagation: by cuttings.
Vigorous shrub; fertilize weekly; cut hard back in autumn and keep rather dry in winter.

☀ ◊◊◊ ✿ 6-11 ❄ 2°C

CESTRUM *newellii*
SOLANACEAE
Propagation: by cuttings.
Slender shrub; very floriferous; fertilize weekly; cut hard back in autumn and keep rather dry in winter.

☀ ◊◊◊ ✿ 5-10 ❄ 2°C

CESTRUM *nocturnum*
SOLANACEAE
Propagation: by cuttings.
Fertilize weekly; if flowering grows less, trim long stem to encourage new flowering; cut hard back in autumn and keep rather dry in winter; scented.

☀ ◊◊◊ ✿ 4-11 ❄ 2°C

CESTRUM *roseum*
SOLANACEAE
Propagation: by cuttings.
Flowers appear earlier than from *C. Newellii*; fertilize weekly; cut hard back in autumn and keep rather dry in winter.

☀ ◊◊◊ ✿ 5-10 ❄ 2°C

CESTRUM *subpulverentum*
SOLANACEAE
Propagation: by cuttings.
Floriferous shrub; fertilize weekly; cut back in autumn and keep rather dry in winter, if necessary in the dark.

☀ ◊◊ ✿ n.v.t. ❄ -25°C

CHAMAECYPARIS *lawsoniana* 'Nana'
CUPRESSACEAE
Pretty spherical-shaped dwarf conifer; yellow leaves; trim from spring to end of summer, but don't cut into older wood.

☀ ◊ ✿ 4-6 ❄ 2°C

CHAMAEROPS *humilis*
PALMAE
Palm; grows little in poor soil, but grows well in fertile soil; may survive a short period of frost; tolerant of drought.

☀ ◊ ✿ 3-5 ❄ 2°C

CHAMELAUCIUM *uncinatum*
MYRTACEAE
Propagation: by cuttings.
Drought-tolerant; fertilize once a month; needs a sandy soil; aromatic foliage; in winter keep rather dry and frost-free.

☀ ◊◊ ✿ 2-3 ❄ -20°C

CHIONODOXA *luciliae*
HYACINTHACEAE
Bulbous perennial; early-flowering and completely hardy; plant bulbs 8 cm deep.

☀ ◊◊ ✿ 5-6 ❄ -8°C

CHOISYA 'Aztec Pride'
RUTACEAE
Propagation: by cuttings.
Evergreen shrub with fragrant flowers; after flowering, cut hard back; the plant will make new shoots in a few weeks; frosthardy; the leaves are smaller than *C. ternata*.

☀ ◊◊ ✿ 5-6 ❄ -8°C

CHOISYA *ternata*
RUTACEAE
Propagation: by cuttings.
Evergreen shrub with fragrant white flowers; if the plant becomes too large, cut back after flowering; it will make new shoots in a few weeks; frosthardy.

☀ ◊◊ ✿ 8-11 ❄ 2°C

CHORISIA *insignis*
BOMBACEAE
Small tree or rather big conservatory plant; very spiny; belongs to the same family as the kapok tree; winter at 2 °C.

☀ ◊◊ ✿ 8-11 ❄ 2°C

CHORISIA *speciosa*
BOMBACEAE
Small tree; sharp spines on the trunks; flowers in autumn, mostly when the tree has lost its foliage; winter at 2 °C.

☀ ◊◊ ✿ n.v.t. ❄ 5°C

CHRYSALIDOCARPUS *lutescens*
PALMAE
Graceful palm; keep rather dry in winter at 10 °C.

☀ ◊◊◊ ✿ 5-11 ❄ 5°C

CHRYSANTHEMUM *frutescens*
COMPOSITAE
Propagation: by cuttings.
Fertilize weekly; cut back in autumn and keep rather dry at 4 °C in winter; syn. *Argyranthemum frutescens*.

☀ ◊◊◊ ✿ 5-11 ❄ 5°C

CHRYSANTHEMUM *frutescens* double
COMPOSITAE
Propagation: by cuttings.
Fertilize weekly; cut back in autumn and keep rather dry at 4 °C in winter; syn. *Argyranthemum frutescens*.

☀ ◊◊◊ ✿ 5-11 ❄ 5°C

CHRYSANTHEMUM *frutescens*
COMPOSITAE
Propagation: by cuttings.
Fertilize weekly; cut back in autumn and keep rather dry at 4 °C during winter; syn. *Argyranthemum frutescens*.

☀ ◊◊◊ ✿ 5-7 ❄ -10°C

CHRYSANTHEMUM *paludosum*
COMPOSITAE
Propagation: by seed.
Fertilize weekly; pretty annual; syn. *Leucanthemum paludosum*.

☼ ◊◊ ✿ 4-10 ❄ 5°C

CITRUS *aurantiacum* var. 'Myrtifolia'
Evergreen; fragrant flowers.

☼ ◊◊ ✿ 4-10 ❄ 5°C

CITRUS X *citrofortunella microcarpa*
Syn. *Citrus mitis*; used for its perfume.

CITRUS
RUTACEAE

Propagation: by cuttings.
Expensive shrubs; not easy to grow; they need a warm and sunny place with plenty of light and moderately soft water; sometimes the plant bears flowers and fruits together; they need a mineral soil; NB: *Citrus* don't like a fertile soil; winter at 5 °C in a light place with plenty of fresh air; water sparingly in winter.

☼ ◊◊ ✿ 4-10 ❄ 5°C

CITRUS *clementine* 'Marie Sol'

☼ ◊◊ ✿ 4-10 ❄ 5°C

CITRUS *kumquat*
The well known kumquat fruit.

☼ ◊◊ ✿ 4-10 ❄ 5°C

CITRUS *limon*

☀ 〇〇 ❀ 4-10 ❄ 5°C

CITRUS *limon* 'Boeddhas Hand'
A sort of lemon; has fingered fruits.

☀ 〇〇 ❀ 4-10 ❄ 5°C

CITRUS *limon* 'Meyer'
Produces lemons throughout the year.

☀ 〇〇 ❀ 4-10 ❄ 5°C

CITRUS
Large shrub.

☀ 〇〇 ❀ 4-10 ❄ 5°C

CITRUS *limon quatre saisons*
Bears fruits throughout the year; somewhat smaller than the common lemon.

☀ 〇〇 ❀ 4-10 ❄ 5°C

☀ 〇〇 ❀ 4-10 ❄ 5°C

CITRUS 'Mandarinier'
Bears large mandarins.

CITRUS *limequat*
A hybrid between kumquat and lemon; very delicious.

☀ ◌◌ ✿ 4-10 ❄ 5°C

CITRUS *medica*

☀ ◌◌ ✿ 4-10 ❄ 5°C

CITRUS *medica* 'Ethrog'
One of the first citrus plants, introduced to the Mediterranean region; used for making crystallised peel.

☀ ◌◌ ✿ 4-10 ❄ 5°C

CITRUS *mitis*
Bears fruit throughout the year; flowers are used in the perfume industry.

☀ ◌◌ ✿ 4-10 ❄ 5°C

CITRUS *pompelo rose*
A vigorous grape-fruit.

☀ ◌◌ ✿ 4-10 ❄ 5°C

CITRUS *piusta*
Named lemon-mandarin.

☀ ◌◌ ✿ 4-10 ❄ 5°C

CITRUS *reticulata* 'Satsuma'
Compact growing shrub with delicious sweet fruits.

☀ ◌◌ ✿ 4-10 ❄ 5°C

CITRUS *reticulata* 'Satsuma'
Fruits.

☀ ◌◌ ✿ 4-10 ❄ 5°C

CITRUS *sinensis* 'Navelate Orange'
Origin unknown; probably South China and Vietnam.

☀ ◌◌ ✿ 4-10 ❄ 5°C

CITRUS *sinensis* 'Navelate'

☀ ◊◊◊ ✾ 5-7   ❄ 0°C

CISTUS **cyprius**
CISTACEAE
Propagation: by cuttings.
Fertilize weekly; early flowering; lovely in spring on the terraces; cut back in autumn and keep rather dry and frost-free in winter.

☀ ◊◊◊ ✾ 5-7   ❄ 0°C

CISTUS **salviifolius**
CISTACEAE
Propagation: by cuttings.
Fertilize weekly; lovely when grown on terraces in spring; cut back in autumn and keep rather dry during winter.

☀ ◊◊ ✾ 4-5   ❄ 2°C

CLEMATIS **cartmanii** 'Joe'
RANUNCULACEAE
Propagation: by cuttings.
Climbing perennial; early flowering; half-hardy; splendid in baskets.

☀ ◊◊ ✾ 6-7   ❄ -5°C

CLEMATIS **forsteri**
RANUNCULACEAE
Propagation: by cuttings.
Climbing perennial; suitable for baskets; could be pruned after flowering.

☀ ◊◊ ✾ 6-9   ❄ -10°C

CLEMATIS 'Diana'
RANUNCULACEAE
Propagation: by cuttings.
Climbing perennial; continuously flowering; in spring, trim untidy stems.

☀ ◊◊ ✾ 6-10   ❄ 4°C

CLEOME **spinosa** 'Cherry Queen'
CAPPARIDACEAE
Propagation: by seed.
Annual; needs sandy, well-drained soil; give plenty of fertilizer; sow at 18 °C in spring; plant out not before May; height 1.20 m.

☀ ◊◊ ✾ 6-10   ❄ 4°C

CLEOME **spinosa** 'Helen Campbell'
CAPPARIDACEAE
See *C. spinosa* 'Cherry Queen'.

☀ ◊◊ ✾ 6-10   ❄ 4°C

CLEOME **spinosa** pink
CAPPARIDACEAE
See *C. spinosa* 'Cherry Queen'.

☀ ◊◊◊ ✾ 5-10   ❄ -10°C

CLERODENDRON **bungei**
VERBENACEAE
Propagation: by cuttings.
Fertilize weekly; when grown outdoors in the garden, nearly hardy; when grown in pots, cut hard back in autumn and keep dry and frost-free during winter; flowers are scented.

☀ ◊◊ ❀ 4-11 ❄ 10°C

CLERODENDRON *fragrans*
VERBENACEAE
Propagation: by cuttings.
Evergreen shrub; flowers throughout the year with white and pink fragrant flowers; probably trim in autumn; keep rather dry at 10 ºC in winter; syn. *C. philippinum.*

☀ ◊◊ ❀ 6-11 ❄ 10°C

CLERODENDRON *paniculatum*
'Starshine'
VERBENACEAE
Propagation: by cuttings.
Evergreen shrub with splendid red-orange flowers in panicles; fertilize freely; if desired, trim in autumn; keep rather dry at 10 ºC during winter.

☀ ◊◊ ❀ 7-11 ❄ 10°C

CLERODENDRON *speciosissimum*
VERBENACEAE
Propagation: by cuttings.
Evergreen shrub with scarlet flowers in panicles; blue berries appear in autumn; cut hard back in autumn and keep rather dry at 10 ºC in winter.

☀ ◊◊ ❀ 6-10 ❄ 10°C

CLERODENDRON *splendens*
VERBENACEAE
Propagation: by cuttings.
Evergreen twining shrub; fertilize regularly; trim long slender stems in autumn; keep rather dry at 10 ºC in winter.

☀ ◊◊ ❀ 6-10 ❄ 10°C

CLERODENDRON *thomsoniae*
VERBENACEAE
Propagation: by cuttings.
Twining climber; height to 4 m; fertilize weekly; needs 14 ºC to survive the winter; in autumn trim long stems; water sparingly in winter.

☀ ◊◊ ❀ 8-11 ❄ -10°C

CLERODENDRON *trichomotum*
VERBENACEAE
Propagation: by cuttings.
Frosthardy shrub; fragrant flowers; blue berries appear in autumn; fertilize regularly; when grown in pots, trim in autumn and keep rather dry and frost-free in winter.

☀️◐ ◌◌ ✿ 6-9 ❄️ 7°C

CLERODENDRON **ugandese**
VERBENACEAE
Propagation: by cuttings.
Fertilize freely; cut hard back in autumn and keep rather dry and frost-free in winter; syn. *C. myricoides* 'Ugandese'; very unusual colour.

☀️◐ ◌◌ ✿ 1-4 ❄️ 7°C

CLERODENDRON **wallichii**
VERBENACEAE
A new variety among the *clerodendrons*; lovely conservatory plant with weeping panicles; fertilize freely; trim after flowering and keep rather dry during its rest period; flowers in winter.

☀️ ◌◌◌ ✿ 4-5 ❄️ 4°C

CLIANTHUS **puniceus**
LEGUMINOSAE
Propagation: by cuttings.
Vigorous climber; fertilize weekly; dead-head; cut hard back in autumn and keep rather dry and frost-free in winter; very striking flower.

☀️◐ ◌◌ ✿ 7-9 ❄️ 7°C

CLITOREA **ternata**
FABACEAE
Propagation: by seeds
Lovely climber that grows to 2 m in height; suitable for indoors; fertilize freely; trim in autumn and keep rather dry and frost-free during winter.

☀️ ◌◌◌ ✿ 8-10 ❄️ 5°C

COBAEA **scandens**
POLEMONIACEAE
Propagation: by seed or cuttings.
Vigorous climber; needs well-drained soil; fragrant; sow at 18 °C; place outdoors not before mid-May; mostly grown as an annual; flowers rather late.

☀️◐ ◌◌ ✿ 6-8 ❄️ 12°C

COFFEA **arabica**
RUBIACEAE
Propagation: by cuttings.
During growing season, give plenty of fertilizer and soft water; water sparingly during winter; can be trained.

☀️◐ ◌◌ ✿ 6-7 ❄️ 10°C

COLEUS **brisana**

☀️◐ ◌◌ ✿ 6-7 ❄️ 10°C

COLEUS 'Meltencave' or 'Aubergine Jewel'

☀️◐ ◌◌ ✿ 6-7 ❄️ 10°C

COLEUS 'Morgenlava'

☀☽ ◌◌ ✿ 6-8 ❄ 10°C

COLEUS 'Ottoman'

☀☽ ◌◌ ✿ 6-8 ❄ 10°C

COLEUS 'Pineapple Beauty'

☀ ◌◌ ✿ 8-9 ❄ 0°C

COLQUHOUNIA *coccinea var. vestita*
LABIATAE/LAMIACEAE
Propagation: by cuttings.
Evergreen shrub for a warm place; in winter, keep rather dry and frost-free.

☀ ◌◌ ✿ 5-6 ❄ 2°C

CONVOLVULUS *cneorum*
CONVOLVULACEAE
Propagation: by cuttings.
Pretty, silver-grey leaves; fertilize weekly; cut back in autumn and winter rather dry at 3 ºC; needs a cold period to get flowers next year.

☀ ◌◌◌ ✿ 4-10 ❄ -5°C

CONVOLVULUS *mauritanicus*
CONVOLVULACEAE
Propagation: by cuttings.
Trailing perennial; fertilize weekly and give plenty of water; easy to grow; no problems surviving the winter; cut back in autumn and keep rather dry at 3 ºC; syn. *C. sabatius*.

☀ ◌◌ ✿ n.v.t. ❄ 5°C

CORDALINE *australis*
AGAVACEAE
Propagation: remove suckers.
Fertilize regularly; young plant can be pinched to encourage branching; water sparingly in winter; remove dry leaves in spring; only very old plants bloom.

☀ ◌◌ ✿ 5 ❄ -5°C

OROKIA *cotoneaster*
ESCALONEACEAE
Propagation: by semi-ripe cuttings in summer.
Intricately-branched shrub; needs well-drained soil; resists some grades of frost; scented flowers.

☀ ◌◌ ✿ 9-3 ❄ 5°C

CORREA 'Mannii'
RUTACEAE
Propagation: by cuttings.
Evergreen shrub; winter-flowering; fertilize weekly; needs soft water and acid soil; syn. *C. Harrisii*; flowers are carmine; inside pink; can be trained.

☀ ◌◌ ✿ 8-11 ❄ 2°C

COSMOS *atrosanguineus*
COMPOSITAE
Chocolate-scented flowers; fertilize weekly; lift the tubers and keep frost-free during winter; replant in spring and give rather high temperature to bud; syn. *Bidens atrosanguineus*.

☀ ◊◊ ❀ 8-9 ❄ 15°C

COSTUS **cuspidatus**
ZINGERACEAE
Propagation: by cuttings.
Fertilize regularly; needs a fertile soil; don't disturb the rootgrowth; keep in a warm, humid place.

☀ ◊ ❀ 8-10 ❄ -2°C

CRASSULA 'Jarcocaule'
CRASSULACEAE
Propagation: by cuttings.
A succulent perennial; half-hardy; needs well-drained soil.

☀ ◊◊◊ ❀ 5-9 ❄ -0°C

CRINUM **powelli**
AMARYLLIDACEAE
Bulbous perennial; fertilize regularly; fragrant; keep moist after flowering; re-pot only when absolutely necessary; the sap of the plant may irritate skin.

☼ ◊◊ ❀ 2-3 ❄ -20°C

CROCUS **tommasinianus** 'Barrs Purple'
IRIDACEAE
Bulbous perennial; flowers very early; is somewhat thinner than C. tomasinianus; increases freely.

☼ ◊◊ ❀ 2-3 ❄ -20°C

CROCUS **tommasinianus**
IRIDACEAE
Bulbous perennial; flowers very early; increases freely.

☼ ◊◊ ❀ 2-3 ❄ -20°C

CROCUS 'Zwanenburg Brons'
IRIDACEAE
Bulbous perennial; early flowering; very suitable for growing in pots.

☼ ◊◊◊ ❀ 7-11 ❄ 2°C

CROTULARIA **agatiflora subsp. imperialis**
LEGUMINOSAE
Propagation: by cuttings.
Cut flower stem hard back after flowering; the plant branches out and will flower again; fertilize weekly; cut hard back in autumn and keep rather dry at 7 °C in winter.

☼ ◊ ❀ 2-11 ❄ 5°C

CRYPTOSTEGIA **grandiflora**
ASCLEPIADACEAE
Propagation: by cuttings.
Freely-branching climber with leathery leaves; flowers appear in axils; cut hard back in autumn; can also be grown as a shrub; keep rather dry in winter.

☼ ◊◊ ❀ 5-11 ❄ 5°C

CUPHEA **celisa**
LYTHRACEAE
Propagation: by cuttings.
Cut back after flowering; the plant will flower again; can flower from early summer until late autumn; cut back in autumn and keep rather dry in winter.

☀ ◊◊◊ ❀ 6-10 ❄ 5°C

CUPHEA *hyssopifolia*
LYTHRACEAE
Propagation: by cuttings.
Fertilize weekly; seen in white, pink and purple colours; cut back in autumn and keep rather dry in winter; easy to grow.

☀ ◊◊◊ ❀ 7-9 ❄ 5°C

CUPHEA *ignea*
LYTHRACEAE
Propagation: by cuttings and seed.
Fertilize weekly; cut back in autumn and keep rather dry and frost-free in winter; the well-known 'Cigar' flower.

☀ ◊◊ ❀ 7-9 ❄ -2°C

CUPHEA *micropetala*
LYTHRACEAE
Propagation: by cuttings.
Compact-growing conservatory plant; fertilize weekly; cut back in autumn and keep rather dry and frost-free in winter.

☀ ◊◊ ❀ 8-10 ❄ 5°C

☀ ◊◊ ❀ 7-9 ❄ 5°C

CUPHEA *species*
LYTHRACEAE
propagation: by cuttings.
Low-growing shrub; fertilize weekly; trim in autumn and keep rather dry and frost-free in winter.

☀ ◊◊ ❀ 7-9 ❄ 5°C

CUPHEA *species*
LYTHRACEAE
Propagation: by cuttings.
Floriferous; fertilize weekly; trim in autumn and keep rather dry and frost-free during winter.

CUPHEA *species*
LYTHRACEAE
Propagation: by cuttings.
Very floriferous; fertilize weekly; cut back in autumn and keep rather dry and frost-free in winter.

☀ ◊◊ ❀ 7-9 ❄ 5°C

CUPHEA species
LYTHRACEAE
Propagation: by cuttings.
Fertilize weekly; cut back in autumn; keep rather dry and frost-free in winter.

☀ ◊◊ ❀ 7-9 ❄ 5°C

CUPHEA species
LYTHRACEAE
Propagation: by cuttings.
Fertilize weekly; cut back in autumn; keep rather dry and frost-free in winter.

☀ ◊◊◊ ❀ 7-9 ❄ -5°C

CURCUMA alisilatifolia
ZINGIBERACEAE
Propagation: by dividing the rhizomes.
Perennial with aromatic (gingery) rhizomes; fertilize weekly; dies back after flowering; keep rather dry and frost-free; replant in February and increase temperature to bud.

☀ ◊ ❀ n.v.t. ❄ 5°C

CYCAS revoluta
CICADECEAE
Sago palm; slow-growing; females produce orange fruits; fertilize sparingly; only older plants will come into flower; keep rather dry at 15 °C in winter; the pith produces sago.

☀ ◊◊◊ ❀ 6 ❄ 5°C

CYPHOMANDRA betacea
SOLANACEAE
Propagation: by cuttings.
Vigorous; grown-up plants need plenty of water; water young plants carefully (too much water leads to leaf drop); fertilize weekly; cut back in autumn; keep rather dry at 10 °C during winter.

☀ ◊◊ ❀ 6 ❄ 5°C

CYPHOMANDRA betacea fruits
SOLANACEAE
Vigorous; called Tree tomato; end of summer the plant produces tomato-like edible fruits; fertilize weekly; cut hard back in autumn; keep rather dry at 10 °C in winter; syn. C. crassicaulis.

☀ ◊◊ ❀ 3-5 ❄ -5°C

CYTISUS canariensis
LEGUMINOSAE
Propagation: by cuttings.
Evergreen, freely branching perennial; young plants have hairy leaves; from the Canarian islands; keep rather dry and frost-free in winter

☀ ◊◊ ❀ 3-5 ❄ -5°C

CYTISUS canariensis survey
LEGUMINOSAE
Syn. C. spachianus and Genista canariensis; fragrant.

☀ ◊◊ ❀ 3-5 ❄ -5°C

CYTISUS 'Porlock'
LEGUMINOSAE
Propagation: by cuttings.
Vigorous conservatory plant with arching stems; fragrant; fertilize weekly; keep rather dry and frost-free in winter.

☀ ◌◌ ✾ 2-5 ❄ 5°C

CYTISUS *x racemosa*
LEGUMINOSAE
Propagation: by cuttings.
Probably a hybrid between *C. canariensis* and *C. maderensis*; fertilize weekly; needs plenty of water; young leaves are hairy; will flower very early under favourable circumstances.

☀ ◌◌◌ ✾ 6-9 ❄ 0°C

DAHLIA 'Bishop of Llandaff'
ASTERACEAE/COMPOSITAE
Propagation: by division of tubers.
Lovely dahlia with very dark foliage; fertilize regularly; in autumn the plant dies off; keep the tubers dry and frost-free; replant in spring.

☀ ◌◌ ✾ 6-8 ❄ 8°C

DALECHAMPIA *dioscoraefolia*
EUPHORBIACEAE
Propagation: by cuttings.
Fertilize weekly; very exclusive plant with striking rose-purple bracts; fragrant; coming on more and more; keep rather dry at 10 ºC in winter.

☀ ◌◌ ✾ 2-4 ❄ -20°C

DAPHNE *mesereum* 'Rubra'
THYMELAECEAE
Propagation: by soft wood-cuttings in summer.
The well known 'Mesereon'; very attractive in pots because of its early bloom; scented flowers are borne before the leaves, followed by lovely fruits.

☀ ◌◌ ✾ 5-6 ❄ -20°C

DIANTHUS
CARYOPHYLLACEAE
Propagation: by division.
Low-growing perennial; very suitable for pots because of its exuberant bloom.

☀ ◌◌ ✾ 6-7 ❄ -20°C

DIANTHUS *barbatus*
CARYOPHYLLACEAE
Propagation: by seed.
'Sweet William'; mostly grown as biennial; when sown in autumn, in bloom the next summer; can survive the winter but is short-living.

☀ ◌◌◌ ✾ 7-9 ❄ 2 °C

DIASCIA
SCROPHULARIACEAE
Propagation: by cuttings.
Lovely creeping perennial; fertilize weekly; cut back in autumn and keep rather dry and frost-free during winter; it is better to begin every year with young plants; many colours available.

☀ ◌◌ ✾ 6-10 ❄ 5°C

DICLIPTERA *suberecta*
ACANTHACEAE
Propagation: by cuttings.
Grey velvety leaves; fertilize weekly; cut hard back after flowering; winter rather dry at 8 ºC; syn. *Justicia suberecta*.

☀ ◌◌◌ ✾ 6-11 ❄ 0°C

DIMEORPHOTECA *aurea*
ASTERACEAE/COMPOSITAE
Propagation: by seed and cuttings.
Mostly grown as annual; fertilize weekly; take cuttings in autumn and throw away old plants; sow seed at 18 ºC.

☀ ◌◌◌ ❀ 3-6 ❄ 5°C

DIOSMA *hirsutum* 'Pink Fountain'
RUTACEAE
Offered in spring because of its early and lasting bloom; cut back long branches in autumn and keep rather dry and frost-free in winter.

☀ ◌ ❀ 5-11 ❄ 10°C

DIPLADENIA *rosea* alba
APOCYNACEAE
Propagation: by cuttings (hard).
Pretty, glossy foliage; slow-growing climber; needs plenty of warmth during winter.

☀ ◌◌ ❀ 6-9 ❄ 2°C

DISSOTIS *canescens*
MELASTOMATACEAE
Propagation: by cuttings.
Conservatory plant with velvety, hairy leaves; fertilize weekly; trim in autumn and keep rather dry at 5 °C in winter; family of the 'Tibouchina'.

☀ ◌◌ ❀ 5-8 ❄ 2°C

DISSOTIS *rotundifolia*
MELASTOMATACEAE
Propagation: by cuttings.
Climbing plant with velvety hairy leaves; cut back in autumn and keep rather dry at 5 °C in winter; family of the 'Tibouchina'.

☀ ◌◌ ❀ 1-4 ❄ 10°C

DOMBEYA *wallichii*
STERCULIACEAE
Propagation: by cuttings.
Vigorous conservatory plant; large leaves; fertilize regularly; trim back in autumn and reduce water; if grown under glass, only trim a little.

☀ ◌◌◌ ❀ 7 ❄ 5°C

DRACAENA *marginata*
AGAVACEAE/DRACAENACEAE
Propagation: by cuttings.
Fertilize regularly; give plenty of water from spring until autumn; water sparingly during winter; small flowers are followed by yellow berries.

☀ ◌◌◌ ❀ 7-10 ❄ 3°C

DURANTA *repens*
VERBENACEAE
Propagation: by cuttings.
Fertilize weekly; cut back blown flowers; vanilla-scented flowers, followed by orange berries in autumn; keep back in autumn and keep rather dry and frost-free in winter.

☀ ◌◌◌ ❀ 7-10 ❄ 3°C

DURANTA *repens* berries
VERBENACEAE
Propagation: by cuttings.
Shrub; fertilize weekly; cut hard back in autumn; keep rather dry and frost-free in winter; syn. *D. plumieri*.

☀ ◌◌◌ ❀ 7-10 ❄ 3°C

DURANTA *repens* alba
VERBENACEAE
Propagation: by cuttings.
Fertilize weekly; cut back blown flowerstems; cut hard back in autumn; keep rather dry and frost-free in winter.

☀ ◊◊◊ ✿ 7-10 ❄ 3°C

DURANTA *repens variegata*
VERBENACEAE
Propagation: by cuttings.
Fertilize weekly; silver, variegated foliage; cut back
blown bloomstems; cut hard back in autumn;
keep rather dry and frost-free during winter.

☀ ◊ ✿ 4-10 ❄ 2°C

DYSCHORISTE *thunbergiflora*
ACANTHACEAE
Propagation: by cuttings.
Pretty conservatory plant with fairly small leaves;
keep rather dry in winter.

☀ ◊◊◊ ✿ 4-6 ❄ -2°C

ECHIUM *fastuosum*
BORAGINACEAE
Propagation: by cuttings.
Pretty plant; needs plenty of space; fertilize weekly; needs well-drained soil; syn. *E. candidans*; keep
rather dry in winter; contact with the leaves may
irritate the skin.

☀ ◊◊ ✿ 6-10 ❄ -3°C

EPILOBIUM *glauca*
ONAGRACEAE
Propagation: by seed.
Invasive annual but can be kept in check easily;
flowers over a long period; fertilize regularly.

☀ ◊◊ ✿ 12-2 ❄ 0°C

ERANTHEMUM *nervosum*
ACANTHACEAE
Propagation: by cuttings.
Pretty perennial, winterblooming; fertilize regu-
larly; needs a well-drained soil; syn. *E. pulchellum*.

☀ ◊◊ ✿ 6-9 ❄ -10°C

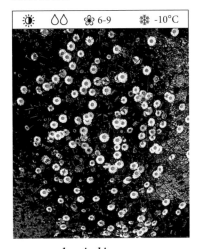

ERIGERON *karvinskianus*
ASTERACEAE/COMPOSITAE
Propagation: by seed.
Invasive annual; can easily be kept in check; fertil-
ize regularly; needs moist, well-drained soil; for
baskets and pots; syn. *E. mucronatus*.

☀ ◊◊ ✿ 9-10 ❄ -5°C

ERIOBOTRYA *japonica*
ROSACEAE
Fragrant flowers and orange apricot-like fruits;
fertilize weekly; if grown in pots keep rather dry
and frost-free during winter; frosthardy when
grown outdoors; 'Loquat'.

☀ ◊◊ ✿ 4-10 ❄ -5°C

ERYSIMUM 'Bowles Mauve'
BRASSICACEAE
Propagation: by cuttings.
Needs well-drained soil; also grows in poor soil; it
is best to take cuttings each year because older
plants become leggy; ideal for borders and pots.

☀ ◊◊ ✿ 6-9 ❄ -5°C

ERYSIMUM 'Bredon'
Propagation: by cuttings.
Needs well-drained soil; take new cuttings each
year; lovely plant; specially for containers.

☀	◊◊	✿ 5-9	❄ -10°C

ERYSIMUM 'Moonlight'
BRASSICACEAE
Propagation: by cuttings.
Creeping perennial; very suitable for containers; produces a carpet of yellow flowers in a few years.

☀	◊◊◊	✿ 6-7	❄ 2°C

ERYTHRINA x bidwillii
LEGUMINOSAE
Propagation: by cuttings.
Vigorous, sparsely-branched conservatory plant; spiny stems; cut hard back in autumn; keep rather dry and frost-free during winter, if necessary in the dark.

☀	◊◊◊	✿ 6-11	❄ 2°C

ERYTHRINA crista-galli
LEGUMINOSAE
Propagation: by cuttings.
Cut back after flowering stems blown, to encourage new shoots to come into bloom; fertilize weekly; cut hard back in autumn; keep rather dry and frost-free during winter.

☀	◊◊	✿ 6-10	❄ 2°C

ERYTHRINA fespatidia
LEGUMINOSAE
Propagation: by cuttings.
Fertilize weekly; red flowers in large racemes; cut hard back in autumn; keep rather dry and frost-free in winter.

☀	◊◊	✿ 5-11	❄ 5°C

ERYTHRINA herbacea
LEGUMINOSAE
Propagation: by cuttings.
Shrub with thick rootstock; fertilize weekly; bright red flowers in large racemes; cut hard back in autumn; keep rather dry and frost-free in winter.

☀	◊◊	✿ 6-7	❄ -2°C

EUCALYPTUS radiata
MYRTACEAE
Propagation: by seed.
Pretty, small tree with very striking flowers; fertilize weekly; needs soft water; keep rather dry and frost-free in winter; fragrant.

EUCOMIS
LILIACEAE

Propagation: by seed or division of the bulbs. Bulbous perennial with unusual florescens; fertilize weekly; dies back in autumn; keep bulbs dry and frost-free; replant in spring; also named 'Pineapple flower' and 'Pineapple lily'.

☼ ◊◊◊ ❀ 6-8 ❄ 0°C

EUCOMIS *bicolor* large plant

☼ ◊◊◊ ❀ 6-8 ❄ 0°C

EUCOMIS hybrid

☼ ◊◊◊ ❀ 6-8 ❄ 0°C

EUCOMIS crème with white

☼ ◊◊◊ ❀ 6-8 ❄ 0°C

EUCOMIS crème

☼ ◊◊◊ ❀ 6-8 ❄ 0°C

EUCOMIS *bicolor*

☼ ◊◊◊ ❀ 6-8 ❄ 0°C

EUCOMIS rose red

☼ ◊◊◊ ❀ 6-8 ❄ 0°C

EUCOMIS rose pale variety

☼ ◊◊◊ ❀ 6-8 ❄ 0°C

EUCOMIS rose

☀ ◇◇◇ ✿ 6-7 ❄ -2°C

EUCALYPTUS *species*
MYRTACEAE
Propagation: by seed.
Pretty, small tree; flowers are very striking; fertilize weekly; needs soft water; keep rather dry and frost-free during winter; fragrant.

☀ ◇◇ ✿ 5-6 ❄ -20°C

EUPHORBIA *cyparissias* 'Fens Ruby'
EUPHORBIACEAE
Propagation: by cuttings or division in spring.
Beautiful perennial; suitable for pots; looks best in a group of plants; needs well-drained soil; normal fertilizer and water.

☀ ◇◇ ✿ 5-6 ❄ -15°C

EUPHORBIA *characias ssp. wulfenii* 'Lambrook Gold'
EUPHORBIACEAE
Propagation: by cuttings or division in spring.
Pretty perennial for pots; eye-catching in a group; needs well-drained soil; normal fertilizer and water.

☀ ◇◇ ✿ 1-3 ❄ 0°C

EUPHORBIA *fulgens* 'Alba'
EUPHORBIACEAE
Propagation: by cuttings.
Easy-to-grow succulent; winter flowering.

☀ ◇◇ ✿ 2-11 ❄ 5°C

EUPHORBIA 'Geroldii' large plant
EUPHORBIACEAE
Crowded, leaved plant; glossy foliage and very floriferous; keep rather dry in winter; one of the best.

☀ ◇◇ ✿ 2-11 ❄ 5°C

EUPHORBIA 'Geroldii'
EUPHORBIACEAE
Succulent perennial; very floriferous; rather dry during winter; splendid.

☀ ◇◇ ✿ 2-6 ❄ 5°C

EUPHORBIA *species*
EUPHORBIACEAE
Splendid perennial; un-named at the moment; a species found in a European botanical garden.

☀ ◇◇◇ ✿ 4-11 ❄ 5°C

EURYOPS *athanasiae*
COMPOSITAE
Propagation: by cuttings.
Fertilize weekly; cut hard back in autumn; keep rather dry at 5 °C during winter; easy plant; *E. athanasiae* has green foliage.

☀ ◇◇◇ ✿ 4-11 ❄ 5°C

EURYOPS *pectinatus*
COMPOSITAE
Propagation: by cuttings.
Fertilize weekly; can be trained as standard; cut hard back in autumn and winter at 5 °C; give plenty of light and fresh air; water moderately; *E. pectinatus* has silver, variegated foliage.

☼ ◌◌◌ ❀ 5-10 ❄ 5°C

FELICIA *ameloides* blue
COMPOSITAE
Propagation: by cuttings.
Fertilize weekly; also available in white; cut back in autumn; keep rather dry and frost-free in winter; easy to make cuttings; start each year with young plants.

☼ ◌◌◌ ❀ 4-10 ❄ 5°C

EURYOPS *virginia*
COMPOSITAE
Propagation: by cuttings.
Fertilize weekly; cut back in autumn and keep rather dry at 5 °C in winter; needs plenty of light and fresh air.

☼ ◌◌◌ ❀ 5-10 ❄ 5°C

FELICIA *ameloides variegata*
COMPOSITAE
Propagation: by cuttings.
Felicia is mostly found with green foliage; we also see *F.* with variegated foliage; fertilize weekly; cut back in autumn; remove old leaves and keep rather dry and frost-free during winter.

☼ ◌◌◌ ❀ 5-10 ❄ 5°C

FELICIA *ameloides variegata alba*
COMPOSITAE
Propagation: by cuttings.
Fertilize weekly; cut hard back in autumn; remove old foliage; keep rather dry and frost-free in winter; during the last years pendant *Felicias* are also offered.

☼ ◌◌◌ ❀ 6-8 ❄ -7°C

FICUS *carica*
MORACEAE
Propagation: by cuttings.
The well known 'Fig'; fertilize weekly; needs well-drained soil; not a reliable hardy; keep frost-free and rather dry in winter; edible fruits appear in October.

☼ ◌◌◌ ❀ 4-11 ❄ -8°C

FREMONTODENDRON *californicum*
STERCULIACEAE
Propagation: by cuttings.
Fertilize weekly; trim back regularly to avoid a leggy plant; keep frost-free and rather dry in winter; easy plant; resists a few grades of frost.

☼ ◊◊ ❀ 4-5 ❄ -10°C

FRITILLARIA *imperialis* 'Lutea'
LILIACEAE
Needs well-drained soil; fertilize regularly; vigorous, bulbous perennial.

☼ ◊◊ ❀ 4-5 ❄ -10°C

FRITILLARIA *imperialis* 'Rubra'
LILIACEAE
Needs well-drained soil; fertilize regularly; vigorous, bulbous perennial.

☼ ◊◊ ❀ 4-5 ❄ -10°C

FRITILLARIA *persica*
LILIACEAE
Needs well-drained soil; fertilize regularly; vigorous.

☼ ◊◊◊ ❀ 6-9 ❄ 2°C

FUCHSIA *arborescens*
ONAGRACEAE
Propagation: by cuttings or seed.
Fertilize weekly; needs well-drained soil; needs a dormant period in winter; keep rather dry and frost-free; lovely blue berries in autumn.

☼ ◊◊◊ ❀ 6-9 ❄ 2°C

FUCHSIA *cordifolia*
ONAGRACEAE
Propagation: by cuttings.
Fertilize weekly; don't trim too much in autumn; even flowers in winter; don't fertilize during winter; give a period of rest in December.

☼ ◊◊◊ ❀ 7-11 ❄ 5°C

FUCHSIA *juntasensis*
ONAGRACEAE
Propagation: by cuttings.
Fertilize weekly; the flowers are followed by splendid orange berries; give a period of rest in winter: water moderately and do not fertilize.

☀ ◊◊◊ ❀ 6-9 ❄ 2°C

FUCHSIA *fulgens rubra grandiflora*
ONAGRACEAE
Propagation: by cuttings.
Fertilize weekly; tuberous plant; keep the tuber dry in peat during winter; replant in spring; could be cut back under glass and wintered at 5 °C.

☀ ◊◊◊ ❀ 6-9 ❄ 5°C

FUCHSIA *procumbens*
ONAGRACEAE
Propagation: by cuttings.
Creeping fuchsia; fertilize weekly; yellow flowers are followed by splendid blue berries; cut back in autumn; keep rather dry and frost-free in winter.

☀ ◊◊ ❀ 2 ❄ -25°C

GALANTHUS *nivalis*
AMARYLLIDACEAE
Bulbous perennial; brightens up the terrace in early spring.

☀ ◊◊◊ ❀ 5-9 ❄ 12°C

GARDENIA *jasminoides*
RUBIACEAE
Propagation: by cuttings.
Fragrant; needs acid soil and soft water; during winter, keep at a temperature not under 12 °C; water regularly and moderately; syn. *G. augusta*.

☀ ◊◊◊ ❀ 5-9 ❄ 12°C

GARDENIA *augusta* 'August B'
RUBIACEAE
Propagation: by cuttings.
Fragrant; fertilize regularly; needs acid soil and soft water; in winter, keep at a temperature not under 12 °C; water regularly and moderately.

☀ ◊◊◊ ❀ 5-9 ❄ 12°C

GARDENIA 'Belmone'
RUBIACEAE
See *G. augusta* 'August B'.

☀ ◊◊◊ ❀ 5-9 ❄ 12°C

GARDENIA 'Coral Gold'
RUBIACEAE
See *G. augusta* 'August B'.

☀ ◊◊◊ ❀ 5-9 ❄ 12°C

GARDENIA 'Miami Supreme'
RUBIACEAE
See *G. augusta* 'August B'.

☀ ◊◊ ❀ 7-9 ❄ -15°C

GAURA *lindheimeri* 'Siskyou Pink'
ONAGRACEAE
Propagation: by division or seed.
Grows splendidly in pots; some months after sowing, the plant will be in bloom; the white form is well known; during a period of abundant rain, place the plant under a shed.

☼ ◊◊◊ ✿ 6-11 ❄ -2°C

GAZANIA
COMPOSITAE
Propagation: by cuttings and seed.
Likes a light, sandy, well-drained soil; sow early
spring; fertilize weekly.

☼ ◊◊◊ ✿ 6-11 ❄ -2°C

GAZANIA red striped
COMPOSITAE
See *Gazania*.

☼ ◊◊◊ ✿ 6-11 ❄ -2°C

GAZANIA
COMPOSITAE
See *Gazania*.

☼ ◊◊◊ ✿ 6-11 ❄ -2°C

GAZANIA
COMPOSITAE
See *Gazania*.

☼ ◊◊◊ ✿ 6-11 ❄ -2°C

GAZANIA
COMPOSITAE
See *Gazania*.

☼ ◊◊◊ ✿ 6-11 ❄ -2°C

GAZANIA
COMPOSITAE
See *Gazania*.

☼ ◊◊◊ ✿ 6-8 ❄ -25°C

GERANIUM *oxonianum* 'Thurstoni-anum'
GERANIACEAE
Propagation: by division.
Perennial, splendid for growing in containers; the
blooms form a dark cloud above the pot.

☼ ◊◊ ✿ n.v.t. ❄ -5°C

GLECHOMA *hederacea variegata*
LABIATAE
Propagation: by cuttings.
Perennial with trailing stems; suitable for containers; flowers are insignificant; fertilize regularly;
keep frost-free during winter; hardy when open-
grown.

☼ ◊◊◊ ✿ 7-9 ❄ 15°C

GLOBBA *winitii*
ZINGIBERACEAE
Propagation: by cuttings.
Needs a warm, humid place and plenty of water
during growing season; in winter keep at a mini-
mum of 15 °C.

GREVILLEA
PROTAECEAE

Propagation: by cuttings and seed.
Striking shrub; flowers – in red or white – seem to creep like spiders along the branches; fertilize moderately and give soft water; trim if necessary but do it before mid-July because after that the buds will be formed for the coming season; during winter keep at a temperature of 5 ºC; do not let the plant dry out.

GREVILLEA *juniperina*

GREVILLEA *longifolia*
Special florescens.

GREVILLEA *longifolia*

GREVILLEA 'Mount Tamboritha'
Compact-growing shrub.

GREVILLEA *rosmarinifolia*
Spreading perennial.

GREVILLEA *rosmarinifolia* 'Alba'
The white G. rosmarinifolia.

GREVILLEA

GREVILLEA

☀ ◌ ✿ 7-12 ❄ 10°C

GLOTTIPHYLLUM *diforme*
AIZOACEAE
Propagation: by cuttings.
During growing season, fertilize with a half gift of
the normal strength; flowering time is in winter;
during rest period, water sparingly.

☀ ◌◌◌ ✿ 7-9 ❄ 5°C

GREWIA *occidentalis*
TILIACEAE
Propagation: by cuttings.
Fertilize weekly during growing season; in winter,
keep temperature between 5 and 10 °C; edible
fruits.

☀ ◌◌ ✿ 4-5 ❄ -5°C

HARDENBERGIA *violaceae* 'Alba'
LEGUMINOSAE
Propagation: by cuttings.
Evergreen climber; keep rather dry during winter.

☀ ◌◌ ✿ 4-5 ❄ -5°C

HARDENBERGIA *violacea*
LEGUMINOSAE
Propagation: by cuttings.
Evergreen climber; keep rather dry in winter.

☀ ◌◌ ✿ 4-5 ❄ -5°C

HARDENBERGIA *violacea* 'Pink
Cascade'
LEGUMINOSAE
Propagation: by cuttings.
Evergreen climber with small racemes of pale pink
flowers; keep rather dry in winter.

☀ ◌◌ ✿ 7-9 ❄ -25°C

HEDERA *helix* 'Arborescens'
ARALIACEAE
Propagation: by cuttings.
Evergreen, creeping ivy; bears berries in autumn;
fully hardy.

☀ ◌◌◌ ✿ 7-9 ❄ 5°C

HEDYCHIUM *coronarium*
ZINGIBERACEAE
Propagation: by division of the rhizome in spring.
Fertilize weekly and give plenty of water; keep the
rhizome dry in winter and at a minimum of 5 °C;
frost-tender; fragrant; White Ginger Lily.

☀ ◌◌◌ ✿ 7-9 ❄ 2°C

HEDYCIUM *gardnerianum*
ZINGIBERACEAE
Propagation: by division of the rhizome in spring.
Fertilize weekly and give plenty of water; winter
the rhizome frost-free and dry; easy.

☀ ◌◌◌ ✿ 7-9 ❄ 0°C

HELICHRYSUM *petiolare*
COMPOSITAE
Propagation: by cuttings.
Grown for its lovely foliage; suitable for baskets;
fertilize weekly; not easy to winter – prone to
moulds (botrytis); take cuttings in spring;
splendid for filling up baskets.

☀ ◊◊ ✿ 7-9 ❄ 0°C

HEBE *andersonii variegata*

☀ ◊◊ ✿ 7-9 ❄ 0°C

HEBE *canterburiensis*

HEBE
SCROPHULARIACEAE

Propagation: by cuttings.
Evergreen shrub; fertilize weekly; winter rather dry; do not let the plant dry out; most are not fully hardy; the larger the foliage, the less hardy the plant.

☀ ◊◊ ✿ 7-9 ❄ 0°C

HEBE *diosmifolia*
Low-growing shrub.

☀ ◊◊ ✿ 7-9 ❄ 0°C

HEBE hybrid

☀ ◊◊ ✿ 7-9 ❄ -0°C

HEBE hybrid

☀ ◊◊ ✿ 7-9 ❄ 0°C

HEBE hybrid

☀ ◊◊ ✿ 7-9 ❄ 0°C

HEBE hybrid

☀ ◊◊ ✿ 7-9 ❄ 0°C

HEBE hybrid

:☼: ◊◊◊ ❀ 7-9 ❄ 0°C

HELICHRYSUM _petiolare_ 'Gold'
COMPOSITAE
Propagation: by cuttings.
Grown for its foliage; fertilize weekly; not easy to
winter – prone to moulds (botrytis); take cuttings
in spring.

:☼: ◊◊◊ ❀ 7-9 ❄ 0°C

HELICHRYSUM _petiolare_ 'Silver'
COMPOSITAE
See _H. petiolare_ 'Gold'.

:☼: ◊◊◊ ❀ 7-9 ❄ 0°C

HELICHRYSUM _microphyllum_
COMPOSITAE
See _H. petiolare_ 'Gold'.

:☼: ◊◊◊ ❀ 4-10 ❄ 5°C

HELIOTROPIUM _amplexicaule_
BORAGINACEAE
Propagation: by cuttings.
Fertilize weekly; keep rather dry and frost-free in
winter.

:☼: ◊◊◊ ❀ 4-10 ❄ 5°C

HELIOTROPIUM _arborescens_
BORAGINACEAE
Propagation: by cuttings.
Fertilize weekly; cut back in autumn and keep
rather dry and frost-free at 10 ºC in winter; fra-
grant; syn. _H. peruvianum_.

:☼: ◊◊◊ ❀ 4-10 ❄ 5°C

HELIOTROPIUM _arborescens_ 'Alba'
BORAGINACEAE
Propagation: by seed or cuttings.
Fertilize weekly; cut back in autumn; keep rather
dry and frost-free in winter; fragrant; syn. _H.
peruvianum_ 'Alba'.

:☼: ◊◊◊ ❀ 2-9 ❄ 5°C

HELIOTROPIUM 'Alba'
BORAGINACEAE
Propagation: by cuttings.
Fertilize weekly; cut back in autumn; keep rather
dry and frost-free in winter; fragrant; early-flow-
ering heliotrope with long racemes of flowers.

:☼: ◊◊ ❀ 12-3 ❄ -20°C

HELLEBORUS _niger_
RANUNCULACEAE
Propagation: by cuttings.
Early-flowering perennial; lovely for containers;
needs well-drained soil; protect from strong cold
winds.

:☼: ◊◊ ❀ 7-9 ❄ -20°C

HEUCHERA 'Rachel'
SAXIFRAGACEAE
Propagation: by division.
Perennial with pretty, coloured and variegated
foliage; evergreen; needs well-drained soil; suit-
able for containers; winter colours.

☼ ◊◊◊ ✿ 6-9 ❄ 5°C

HIBISCUS hybrid

☼ ◊◊◊ ✿ 6-9 ❄ 5°C

HIBISCUS hybrid

HIBISCUS
MALVACEAE

Propagation: by cuttings.
If they are not sprayed to prevent growth, all kinds of *hibiscus* grow well outdoors and there are very special colours and shapes; fertilize weekly; keep in a light and warm place; cut back in autumn and keep rather dry at 10 °C during winter; do not bring them outdoors too early; bud drop will be caused by a big change in temperature.

☼ ◊◊◊ ✿ 6-9 ❄ 5°C

HIBISCUS hybrid

☼ ◊◊◊ ✿ 6-9 ❄ 5°C

HIBISCUS hybrid

☼ ◊◊◊ ✿ 6-9 ❄ 5°C

HIBISCUS hybrid

☀ ◊◊◊ ❀ 6-9   ❄ 5C

☀ ◊◊◊ ❀ 6-9   ❄ 5°C

HIBISCUS *acetosella*

HIBISCUS hybrid

☀ ◊◊◊ ❀ 6-9   ❄ 5°C

HIBISCUS double 'Mini Skirt'

☀ ◊◊◊ ❀ 6-9   ❄ 5°C

☀ ◊◊◊ ❀ 6-9   ❄ 5°C

☀ ◊◊◊ ❀ 6-9   ❄ 5°C

HIBISCUS 'Charles September'

HIBISCUS 'Geisha'

HIBISCUS 'Janys'

☼ ◊◊◊ ✿ 6-9 ❄ 5°C

HIBISCUS 'Jim Hendry'

☼ ◊◊◊ ✿ 6-9 ❄ 5°C

HIBISCUS 'Mystic Pink'

☼ ◊◊◊ ✿ 6-9 ❄ 5°C

HIBISCUS *coccineus*

☼ ◊◊◊ ✿ 6-9 ❄ 5°C

HIBISCUS *geranoides*

☼ ◊◊◊ ✿ 6-9 ❄ 5°C

HIBISCUS *moscheutos subsp. palustris*

☼ ◊◊◊ ✿ 6-9 ❄ 5°C

HIBISCUS *mutabilis*

☼ ◊◊◊ ✿ 6-9 ❄ 5°C

HIBISCUS *rosa chinensis*

☼ ◊◊◊ ✿ 6-9 ❄ 5°C

HIBISCUS *trionum*

☼ ◊◊◊ ✿ 6-9 ❄ 5°C

HIBISCUS *schizopetalus*

☀ ◌◌ ❀ 7-9 ❄ -20°C

HEUCHERA 'Stormy Seas'
SAXIFRAGACEAE
Propagation: by division.
Perennial with pretty, coloured and variegated foliage; suitable for containers; evergreen; needs well-drained soil; winter colours.

☀ ◌◌◌ ❀ 4-7 ❄ 0°C

HIBBERTIA *scandens*
DILLENIACEAE
Propagation: by cuttings.
Vigorous climber; tolerant of heat but needs plenty of water; fertilize weekly; if necessary, cut back in autumn; keep rather dry and frost-free in winter.

☀ ◌ ❀ 7-9 ❄ 5°C

HOLMSKIOLDIA *sanguinea*
VERBENACEAE
Propagation: by cuttings.
Evergreen climber; fertilize weekly; trimming back after flowering keeps the plant compact; winter rather dry and frost-free.

☀ ◌◌◌ ❀ 7-8 ❄ -25°C

HOSTA 'Blue Cadet'
FUNKIACEAE
Propagation: by division.
Perennial; suitable for containers; fertilize weekly; winter frost-free when grown in pots; fully hardy when grown outdoors; attractive to snails.

☀ ◌◌◌ ❀ 7-9 ❄ -25°C

HOSTA *fortunei* 'Patriot'
FUNKIACEAE
See H. 'Blue Cadet'.

☀ ◌◌◌ ❀ 7-9 ❄ -25°C

HOSTA *sieboldii* 'Snowflake'
FUNKIACEAE
See H. 'Blue Cadet'.

☀ ◌◌◌ ❀ 7-8 ❄ -25°C

HOSTA 'Wide Brim'
FUNKIACEAE
See H. 'Blue Cadet'.

☀ ◌◌◌ ❀ 7-9 ❄ -25°C

HOSTA
FUNKIACEAE
See H. 'Blue Cadet'.

☀ ◌◌◌ ❀ 6-10 ❄ 0°C

HYDRANGEA *macrophylla* hybrid
HYDRANGEACEAE
Old-fashioned perennial that now makes an interesting come-back; fertilize weekly; in acid soil, the blooms are blue and in chalk soil, the blooms are pink or red; when grown in pots, keep frost-free in winter; water moderately.

☀ ◌◌◌ ❀ 3-10 ❄ 6°C

IMPATIENS hybrid

☀ ◌◌◌ ❀ 3-10 ❄ 6°C

IMPATIENS hybrid

IMPATIENS
BALSEMINACEAE

Propagation: by seed or cuttings.
Annual; in spring, offered in many colours; last years all sorts of botanical *impatiens* came onto the market; fertilize weekly and water well; it is better to take cuttings in spring rather than keeping the plant.

☀ ◌◌◌ ❀ 3-10 ❄ 6°C

IMPATIENS hybrid

☀ ◌◌◌ ❀ 3-10 ❄ 6°C

IMPATIENS white

☀ ◌◌◌ ❀ 3-10 ❄ 6°C

IMPATIENS firefly purple

☀ ◊◊◊ ❀ 3-10 ❄ 6°C

IMPATIENS firefly white

☀ ◊◊◊ ❀ 3-10 ❄ 6°C

IMPATIENS 'Lavender Orchid'

☀ ◊◊◊ ❀ 3-10 ❄ 6°C

IMPATIENS 'Nieuw Guinea'

☀ ◊◊◊ ❀ 3-10 ❄ 6°C

IMPATIENS 'Nieuw Guinea'

☀ ◊◊◊ ❀ 3-10 ❄ 6°C

☀ ◊◊◊ ❀ 3-10 ❄ 6°C

IMPATIENS sparkler rose

IMPATIENS sparkler red

☀️ ◐◐◐ 🌼 3-10   ❄️ 6°C

IMPATIENS salsa red

☀️ ◐◐◐ 🌼 3-10   ❄️ 6°C

IMPATIENS *niamniamensis*

☀️ ◐◐◐ 🌼 3-10   ❄️ 6°C

IMPATIENS *niamniamensis* 'Congo Cockatoo'

☀️ ◐◐◐ 🌼 3-10   ❄️ 6°C

IMPATIENS species

☀️ ◐◐◐ 🌼 3-10   ❄️ 6°C

IMPATIENS *velvetea*

☀️ ◐◐◐ 🌼 3-10   ❄️ 6°C

MPATIENS *velvetea* 'Secret Love'

☀ ◊◊◊ ✿ 6-10 ❄ 0°C

HYDRANGEA *macrophylla* hybrid
HYDRANGEACEAE
Old-fashioned perennial but today very popular; fertilize weekly; in acid soil the blooms are blue; in chalk soil they are pink or red; when grown in pots keep frost-free in winter; water moderately.

☀ ◊◊◊ ✿ 7-10 ❄ 5°C

IOCHROMA *coccineum*
SOLANACEAE
Propagation: by cuttings.
Evergreen shrub; fertilize weekly; cut hard back in autumn and keep rather dry and frost-free in winter, in the dark if necessary; trim again in spring.

☀ ◊◊◊ ✿ 7-10 ❄ 5°C

IOCHROMA *cyaneum*
SOLANACEAE
Propagation: by cuttings.
Fertilize weekly; cut hard back in autumn and keep rather dry and frost-free in winter, in the dark if necessary; trim again in spring and pot on.

☀ ◊◊◊ ✿ 7-10 ❄ 5°C

IOCHROMA *grandiflorum* light variety
SOLANACEAE
Propagation: by cuttings.
Evergreen shrub; fertilize weekly; cut hard back in autumn; keep rather dry and frost-free in winter, if necessary in the dark; trim again in spring and pot on.

☀ ◊◊◊ ✿ 7-10 ❄ 5°C

IOCHROMA *purpureum*
SOLANACEAE
Propagation: by cuttings.
Fertilize weekly; cut hard back in autumn; keep rather dry and frost-free in winter, if necessary in dark; origin is uncertain but some authors consider that it is a colour variant of the *I. cyaneum*.

☀ ◊◊◊ ✿ 7-10 ❄ 5°C

IOCHROMA *warscewiczii*
SOLANACEAE
Propagation: by cuttings.
Fertilize weekly; cut hard back in autumn; keep rather dry and frost-free in winter, in the dark if necessary; in spring trim somewhat and pot on.

☀ ◊◊◊ ✿ 6-9 ❄ 5°C

IPOMOEA *alba*
CONVOLVULACEAE
Propagation: by seed.
Fertilize weekly; fragrant flowers that open at night; vigorous climber.

☀ ◊◊◊ ✿ 4-10 ❄ 5°C

IPOMOEA *fistulosa*
CONVOLVULACEAE
Propagation: by cuttings.
Twining perennial; fertilize weekly; trim long branches in autumn; keep rather dry at 7 °C in winter.

☀ ◊◊◊ ✿ 7-9 ❄ 5°C

IPOMOEA *indica* large plant
CONVOLVULACEAE

☀ ◊◊◊ ❀ 7-9 ❄ 5°C

IPOMOEA **indica**
CONVOLVULACEAE
Propagation: by cuttings.
Climbing perennial; trim long branches and keep
rather dry and frost-free in winter.

☀ ◊◊◊ ❀ 6-8 ❄ 2°C

IPOMOEA **leari**
CONVOLVULACEAE
Propagation: by cuttings.
Climbing perennial; fertilize weekly; deciduous;
trim long branches; keep rather dry at 5 °C.

☀ ◊◊◊ ❀ 6-9 ❄ 10°C

IPOMOEA **mauritiana**
CONVOLVULACEAE
Propagation: by cuttings.
Vigorous climber with rhizomes; needs fertile
soil; winter in a warm place; grows in humid sub-
tropical forests.

☀ ◊◊◊ ❀ 7-9 ❄ 6°C

IPOMOEA **purpurea**
CONVOLVULACEAE
Propagation: by cuttings.
Twining perennial; fertilize weekly; trim in
autumn and keep rather dry and frost-free during
winter.

☀ ◊◊◊ ❀ 6-11 ❄ 5°C

ISOPLEXIS **isabelliana**
SCROPHURALIACEAE
Propagation: by cuttings.
Fertilize weekly; after flowering cut back the
flower-stem as low as possible to get a bushy plant;
don't cut back in autumn; keep rather dry at 7 °C
in winter.

☀ ◊◊◊ ❀ 6-11 ❄ 5°C

ISOPLEXIS **canariensis**
SCROPHURALIACEAE
Propagation: by cuttings.
Fertilize weekly; cut back the flower-stem after
flowering to get a bushy plant; don't cut back in
autumn; keep rather dry at 7 °C.

☀ ◊◊ ❀ 6-11 ❄ 0°C

ISOTOMA **axillaris**
CAMPANULACEAE
Propagation: by cuttings.
Fertilize weekly; cut back in autumn and keep
rather dry and frost-free during winter; best
results are with new cuttings each year; syn. *Lau-
rentia axilaris*; leaves are poisonous.

☀ ◊◊◊ ❀ 6-10 ❄ 2°C

ISOTOMA **longiflora**
CAMPANULACEAE
Propagation: by cuttings.
Fertilize weekly; cut back in autumn and keep
rather dry and frost-free during winter; syn. *Lau-
rentia longiflora*; very poisonous.

☀ ◊◊◊ ❀ 5-9 ❄ 10°C

IXORA **coccinea**
RUBIACEAE
Propagation: by cuttings.
Needs well-drained soil; fertilize twice during
growing season and give plenty of water; in
winter, water sparingly and keep at a temperature
of 8 °C.

☼ ◑ ◊◊◊ ✿ 5-9 ❄ 10°C

IXOARA 'Candy Pink'
RUBIACEAE
Propagation: by cuttings.
Needs well-drained soil; fertilize twice during growing season and give plenty of water; during winter, water sparingly and keep at 8 °C.

☼ ◊◊ ✿ 6-10 ❄ 8°C

JACOBINEA *carnea alba*
ACANTHACEAE
Propagation: by cuttings.
Fertilize weekly; cut back the flower-stem after flowering to get a bushy plant; don't cut back in autumn; keep rather dry at 10 °C in winter; syn. *Justicia carnea alba*.

☼ ◊◊ ✿ 6-10 ❄ 8°C

JACOBINEA *carnea*
ACANTHACEAE
Propagation: by cuttings.
Fertilize weekly; after flowering, cut back the flower-stem to get a bushy plant; don't cut back in autumn; syn. *Justicia carnea*.

☼ ◊◊ ✿ 4-6 ❄ 8°C

JACOBINEA 'Mohintii'
ACANTHACEAE
Propagation: by cuttings.
Fertilize weekly; cut back the flower-stem after flowering to get a bushy plant; don't cut back in autumn; keep rather dry at 10 °C in winter.

☼ ◊◊ ✿ 6-8 ❄ 5°C

JACOBINEA *species*
ACANTHACEAE
Propagation: by cuttings.
Fertilize weekly; cut back the flower-stem after flowering; don't cut back in autumn; keep rather dry at 10 °C in winter.

☼ ◊◊ ✿ 12-3 ❄ 10°C

JACOBINEA *pauciflora*
ACANTHACEAE
Propagation: by cuttings.
Fertilize weekly; trim long branches; don't cut back in autumn; keep rather dry at 10 °C in winter; syn. *Justicia rizzinii*; winterbloomer.

☀️◐ 💧💧💧 ✿ 3-5 ❄️ 10°C

JACOBINEA **velutina**
ACANTHACEAE
Propagation: by cuttings.
Fertilize weekly; cut back flower-stems after flowering to get a bushy plant; don't cut back in autumn; keep rather dry at 10 °C in winter; syn. *Justicia velutina*.

☀️ 💧💧 ✿ 4-10 ❄️ 0°C

JASMINUM **angulare**
OLEACEAE
Propagation: by cuttings.
Fragrant climber; fertilize weekly; keep rather dry and frost-free in winter.

☀️ 💧💧 ✿ 4-10 ❄️ -2°C

JASMINUM **azoricum**
OLEACEAE
Propagation: by cuttings.
Fragrant climber; evergreen; fertilize weekly; keep rather dry and frost-free in winter.

☀️ 💧💧 ✿ 2-4 ❄️ -8°C

JASMINUM **mesnyi**
OLEACEAE
Propagation: by cuttings.
Fragrant climber; fertilize weekly; frosthardy up to -8 °C; winter rather dry in a sheltered place.

☀️◐ 💧💧 ✿ 3-12 ❄️ 0°C

JASMINUM **nitidum**
OLEACEAE
Propagation: by cuttings.
Well-branching shrub; fragrant; fertilize weekly; trim long branches; keep rather dry and frost-free in winter.

☀️◐ 💧💧 ✿ 2-4 ❄️ 8°C

JASMINUM **officinale**
OLEACEAE
Propagation: by cuttings.
Pretty climber; fertilize weekly; fragrant; trim long branches; keep rather dry in winter at 8 °C; easy-to-grow.

☀️◐ 💧💧 ✿ 1-4 ❄️ 8°C

JASMINUM **polyanthum**
OLEACEAE
Propagation: by cuttings.
Pretty climber; pink buds and white fragrant flowers; trim long branches; keep rather dry in winter at 8 °C; easy-to-grow.

☀️ 💧💧 ✿ 6-8 ❄️ -10°C

JASMINUM **revolutum**
OLEACEAE
Propagation: by cuttings.
Well-branching shrub; lightly scented; fertilize weekly; frosthardy; winter rather dry in a sheltered place.

☀️ 💧💧 ✿ 3-10 ❄️ 0°C

JASMINUM **sambac**
OLEACEAE
Propagation: by cuttings.
Fragrant climber; fertilize weekly; keep rather dry and frost-free in winter; used to make jasmin tea.

☼ ◊◊ ✿ 6-8 ❄ 2°C

JASMINUM *sambac* 'Grand Duke of Toscane'
OLEACEAE
Propagation: by cuttings.
Small shrub with very fragrant double flowers; fertilize weekly; flower fades from white to purple; rare.

☼ ◊◊ ✿ 6-8 ❄ 5°C

JATROPHA *integerrima*
EUPHORBIACEAE
Propagation: by cuttings.
Fertilize regularly; give a dry period in winter; needs 8 °C in winter; needs more water in summer and plenty of warmth.

☼ ◊◊◊ ✿ 6-8 ❄ 5°C

JATROPHA *podagrica*
EUPHORBIACEAE
Propagation: by cuttings.
Fertilize regularly; needs a dry period in winter at 10 °C; needs plenty of water and warmth in summer; easy to grow.

☼ ◊ ✿ 7-11 ❄ 10°C

JUANULLOA *aurantiaca*
SOLANACEAE
Propagation: by cuttings.
Grows in rainforests as an epiphyt; fertilize weekly; needs well-drained soil and little water; winter in a warm place; trim in spring; syn. *J. Mexicana*.

☼ ◊◊ ✿ 4-5 ❄ 2°C

JUSTICIA *spicigera*
ACANTHACEAE
Propagation: by cuttings.
Well-branching shrub; keep rather dry and frost-free in winter.

☼ ◊◊◊ ✿ 8-9 ❄ 5°C

KENNEDIA *coccinea*
LEGUMINOSAE
Propagation: by cuttings.
Poorly-flowering climber but very striking; fertilize weekly; trim long branches in autumn; keep rather dry at 5 °C in winter; syn. *K. Rubicunda*.

☼ ◊◊◊ ✿ 4-7 ❄ 5°C

KENNEDIA *nigricans*
LEGUMINOSAE
Propagation: by cuttings.
Climber; fertilize weekly; needs sandy soil; vigorous; trim back long branches in autumn; keep rather dry and frost-free in winter.

☼ ◊◊ ✿ 7-8 ❄ -15°C

KITAIBELIA *vitifolia*
MALVACEAE
Propagation: by seed.
Needs not too fertile a soil; splendid as solitary; attractive to bees and butterflies.

☼ ◊ ✿ 8-9 ❄ 0°C

LAGERSTROEMIA dwarf variety
LYTHRACEAE
Propagation: by cuttings.
Late-flowering; fertilize weekly; requires plenty of warmth in summer for good flowering; intolerant of a long period of rain; cut hard back in autumn; keep rather dry and frost-free in winter.

☀ ◊ ✿ 8-9 ❄ 0°C

LAGERSTROEMIA *indica* pink
LYTHRACEAE
Propagation: by cuttings.
Late-flowering; fertilize weekly; requires plenty of warmth during summer for good flowering; cut hard back in autumn (for good flowering next year); keep rather dry and frost-free in winter.

☀ ◊ ✿ 8-9 ❄ 0°C

LAGERSTROEMIA *indica* red
LYTHRACEAE Propagation: by cuttings.
Late-flowering; fertilize weekly; requires plenty of warmth for good flowering; intolerant to long periods of rainfall; cut hard back in autumn (for better flowering next year) and keep rather dry and frost-free in winter.

☀ ◊ ✿ 8-9 ❄ 0°C

LAGERSTROEMIA 'Little Chief'
LYTHRACEAE
Propagation: by cuttings.
Late-flowering; requires plenty of warmth for good flowering; intolerant to a long period of rainfall; cut hard back in autumn; keep rather dry and frost-free in winter.

☀ ◊◊◊ ✿ 6-8 ❄ 0°C

LAGUNARIA *patersonii*
MALVACEAE
Propagation: by cuttings.
Fertilize weekly; after flowering, fruits appear; do not remove these before autumn; trim in autumn and keep rather dry at 4 °C in winter.

◐ ◊ ✿ 6-12 ❄ 5°C

LAPAGERIA *rosea*
LILIACEAE
Propagation: by cuttings.
Slow-growing climber; well-flowering as older plant; waxy flowers; fertilize weekly; don't cut back before winter; water sparingly; easy to winter.

☀ ◊◊ ✿ 2-4 ❄ -2°C

LAURUS *nobilis**
LAURACEAE
Propagation: by cuttings.
The well-known 'Sweet Laurel'; green-yellow flowers followed, on female plants, by black berries; aromatic leaves; fertilize regularly; keep rather dry and frost-free in winter.

☀ ◊◊◊ ✿ 7-9 ❄ -10°C

LAVATERA 'Barnsley'
MALVACEAE
Propagation: by cuttings.
Fertilize weekly; requires not too fertile a soil, which results in many leaves and little bloom; frost-hardy; when grown in pots, cut back in autumn and winter rather dry and frost-free.

☀ ◊◊◊ ✿ 7-9 ❄ 0°C

LAVATERA *maritima*
MALVACEAE
Propagation: by cuttings.
Fertilize weekly; cut back in autumn and keep rather dry and frost-free in winter; syn. *L. bicolor*.

☀ ◊◊ ✿ 5-9 ❄ -10°C

LAVANDULA *angustifolia* 'Alba'
LABIATAE
Propagation: by cuttings.
Scented shrub; fertilize weekly; when grown in pot trim early autumn and keep rather dry and frost-free during winter; when grown outdoors, fully hardy.

LANTANA
VERBENACEAE

Propagation: by cuttings.
Lantana camara is an evergreen perennial often offered as shrub or standard; new colours and colour combinations appear regularly; after flowering, lovely blue berries appear; to get the plant flowering, remove the berries; fertilize weekly; cut hard back in autumn and keep rather dry and frost-free in winter; all parts of the plant should be poisonous.
Lantana montevidensis is a spreading shrub; lovely in baskets and in front of window boxes; fertilize weekly; cut hard back in autumn and keep rather dry and frost-free in winter; *lantanas* are attractive to butterflies!

LANTANA *sellowiana* 'Alba'

LANTANA *camara* hybrid

LANTANA *camara* hybrid

LANTANA *camara* hybrid

LANTANA *camara* hybrid

LANTANA *camara* 'Butterfly'

LANTANA *camara* 'Cupfer Riese'

LANTANA *camara* 'Goldsonne'

☀ ◊◊◊ ✿ 6-10 ❄ 5°C

LANTANA *camara* 'Ingelsheimer'

☀ ◊◊◊ ✿ 6-10 ❄ 5°C

LANTANA *camara* 'Niobe'

☀ ◊◊◊ ✿ 6-10 ❄ 5°C

LANTANA *camara* 'Old Rose'

☀ ◊◊◊ ✿ 6-10 ❄ 5°C

LANTANA *camara* 'Slot Ortenburg'

☀ ◊◊◊ ✿ 6-10 ❄ 5°C

LANTANA *montevidensis* white

LANTANA *montevidensis* lavender

☼ ◊◊ ✿ 2-4 ❄ -20°C

LAVANDULA **dentata**
LABIATAE
Propagation: by cuttings.
Scented shrub; fertilize weekly; when grown in pots, trim early autumn and keep rather dry and frost-free in winter; when grown outdoors, fully hardy.

☼ ◊◊ ✿ 5-9 ❄ 0°C

LAVANDULA **stoechas**
LABIATAE
Propagation: by cuttings.
Scented shrub; fertilize weekly; trim before the winter and keep frost-free; water sparingly; half hardy.

☼ ◊◊◊ ✿ 8-10 ❄ 0°C

LEONOTIS **leonuris**
LABIATAE
Propagation: by cuttings.
Flowers late; the vivid orange flowers are very striking; fertilize weekly; cut hard back in autumn; keep rather dry and frost-free during winter; syn. *L. oxymifolia*.

☼ ◊ ✿ 4-7 ❄ 5°C

LEPTOSPERMUM **scoparium** double, light pink
MYRTACEAE
Propagation: by cuttings.
Needs acid soil, as all plants of the *myrte* family; give soft water; only trim to get a better shape; keep rather dry and frost-free in winter.

☼ ◊ ✿ 4-7 ❄ 5°C

LEPTOSPERMUM **scoparium** 'Red Dam'
MYRTACEAE
See *L. scoparium* pale rose double.

☼ ◊ ✿ 4-7 ❄ 5°C

LEPTOSPERMUM **scoparium** pink
MYRTACEAE
See *L. scoparium* light rose double.

☼ ◊◊ ✿ 5-9 ❄ -10°C

LEPTOSPERMUM **scoparium** double, very dark red
See *L. scoparium* light rose double.

☼ ◊◊ ✿ 9-10 ❄ -15°C

LESPEDEZA **thunbergii**
LEGUMINOSAE
Propagation: by cuttings.
Arching shrub; trim in autumn; winter rather dry and frost-free; late to bloom.

☼ ◊◊ ✿ 8-9 ❄ 0°C

LEUCAENA **leucocephala**
LEGUMINOSAE
Propagation: by cuttings.
Fertilize weekly; the feathered leaves close at night; scented flowers; winter rather dry.

☀️◐ ◊◊ ❀ 7-8 ❄️ -10°C

LEUCOTHOE *axillaris*
ERICACEAE
Propagation: by division.
Evergreen; needs well-drained acid soil; lovely displayed in pots in winter; keep in a shady place.

☀️ ◊◊ ❀ 7-8 ❄️ -10°C

LEUCOTHOE *walteri* 'Rainbow'
ERICACEAE
Propagation: by cuttings.
Needs well-drained acid soil; suitable for pots in winter; pretty, coloured foliage; keep in a shady place.

☀️ ◊◊ ❀ 5-7 ❄️ -10°C

LIBERTIA *grandiflora*
IRIDACEAE
Propagation: by division of the rhizome.
Needs well-drained soil; fertilize weekly; frosthardy; protect from severe cold.

☀️ ◊◊◊ ❀ 6-7 ❄️ -8°C

LIGUSTRUM *delavayanum*
OLEACEAE
Propagation: by cuttings.
Fertilize weekly; needs well-drained soil; in autumn bears lovely berries; frosthardy; protect from severe cold.

☀️ ◊◊◊ ❀ 7-9 ❄️ 2°C

☀️ ◊◊ ❀ 4-6 ❄️ -5°C

LILIUM
LILIACEAE
Fertilize weekly; bulbous perennial; prefers full sun with the base of the plant in shade; dies back after flowering; keep rather dry and replant in autumn.

LIGUSTRUM *japonicum texanum*
OLEACEAE
Propagation: by cuttings.
Fertilize weekly; can be trained into shape; fragrant; keep rather dry and frost-free in winter; can be trimmed if necessary.

☀   ◊◊   ✿ 4-6   ❄ -5°C

LILIUM*
LILIACEAE
Fertilize weekly; bulbous perennial; prefers full
sun with the base of the plant in shade; dies back
after flowering; keep rather dry and replant in
autumn.

☀   ◊◊◊   ✿ 7-9   ❄ -8°C

LIMNANTHUS *douglasii*
LIMNANTHACEAE
Propagation: by seed.
Fertilize weekly; the scented flowers are attractive
to bees and butterflies; plants sown in autumn
must be protected from frost.

☀   ◊◊   ✿ 6-9   ❄ -8°C

LINARIA *purpurea*
SCROPHULARIACEAE
Propagation: by seed.
Fertilize regularly; pinch out the top to encourage
a bushy plant; seeds spontaneously, but not inva-
sive.

☀◑   ◊◊   ✿ 7-8   ❄ -20°C

LIRIOPE *spicata*
CONVALLARIACEAE
Propagation: by cuttings.
Perennial; suitable for containers; fertilize weekly.

☀   ◊◊◊   ✿ 5-8   ❄ -5°C

LOBELIA *erinus* 'Cambridge Blue'
CAMPANULACEAE/LOBELIACEAE
Propagation: by seed.
Fertilize weekly; needs well-drained soil; in many
shades of blue, pink and white.

☀   ◊◊◊   ✿ 6-7   ❄ 0°C

LOBELIA *eulalia* 'Berridge'
CAMPANULACEAE/LOBELIACEAE
Propagation: by cuttings or division.
Fertilize weekly; after flowering, young plants
appear around the old plant; in autumn the old
plant dies back; keep rather dry and frost-free in
winter.

☀   ◊   ✿ 5-10   ❄ 0°C

LOESELIA *mexicana*
POLEMONIACEAE
Propagation: by cuttings.
Needs a sandy soil; remove old flowers to prevent
diseases; keep rather dry and frost-free in winter.

☀   ◊◊◊   ✿ 5-10   ❄ 5°C

LOTUS *berthelotii*
LEGUMINOSAE
Propagation: by cuttings.
Fertilize weekly; trim back long slender stems in
summer; cut hard back in autumn and keep rather
dry in winter; needs a cold period to get in bloom
the next year; basket-plant.

☀   ◊◊◊   ✿ 5-10   ❄ 5°C

LOTUS *berthelotii* 'Gold'
LEGUMINOSAE
Propagation: by cuttings.
Trailing perennial; fertilize weekly; trim long
stems in summer; cut hard back in autumn; keep
rather dry and frost-free in winter; needs a cold
period to get flowers in the next year.

LOTUS *jacobeus*
LEGUMINOSAE
Propagation: by cuttings.
Fertilize weekly; needs plenty of water and full sun; trim in autumn and keep rather dry and frost-free in winter.

LOTUS *nigrescens*
LEGUMINOSAE
Propagation: by cuttings.
Fertilize weekly; needs plenty of water and full sun; cut back in autumn; keep rather dry and frost-free in winter.

LYCHNIS *coronaria*
CARYOPHYLLACEAE
Propagation: by division.
Fertilize regularly; pretty, grey foliage; the well-known 'Dusty Miller'.

LYSIMACHIA *nummularia*
PRIMULACEAE
Propagation: by division.
Fertilize normally; invasive; hardy.

MAHONIA *japonica**
BERBERIDACEAE
After flowering, splendid blue berries appear; because of the early flowers, very attractive for growing in containers; when grown in pots, fertilize regularly.

MALVASTRUM *lateritia*
MALVACEAE
Propagation: by cuttings.
Low-growing perennial; splendid for pots; fertilize weekly; when grown in pots, protect from severe frost.

MALVAVISCUS *arboreus var. arboreus*
MALVACEAE
Propagation: by cuttings.
Fertilize weekly; to get flowers throughout the season, trim once during growing season; cut hard back in autumn; keep rather dry at 7 ºC during winter.

MALVAVISCUS *arboreus var. penduliflorus*
MALVACEAE
Propagation: by cuttings.
Fertilize weekly; pendant flowers; to get flowers throughout the season, trim once during growing season; cut hard back in autumn and keep rather dry at 7 ºC in winter.

MALVAVISCUS *arboreus var. penduliflorus alba*
MALVACEAE
Propagation: by cuttings.
Fertilize weekly; to get flowers throughout the season, trim once during the growing season; cut hard back in autumn and keep rather dry at 7 ºC in winter.

☀ ◌◌ ❀ 5-10 ❄ 5°C

MANDEVILLA 'Alice du Pont'
Do not cut back in autumn and keep rather dry at 5 °C; splendid for containers; named after the family du Pont, Pennsylvania, from where the plant comes.

☀ ◌◌ ❀ 5-10 ❄ 5°C

MANDEVILLA *amabilis*

MANDEVILLA
APOCYNACEAE

Propagation: by cuttings.
Fertilize weekly; cut somewhat back in autumn; keep rather dry at 5 °C in winter; an eyecatcher; suitable to be trained along a pillar of wire-netting.

☀ ◌◌ ❀ 5-10 ❄ 5°C

MANDEVILLA *boliviensis*
Slow-growing climber; trim somewhat in autumn and winter at 10 °C; difficult to make cuttings from it.

☀ ◌◌ ❀ 5-10 ❄ 5°C

MANDEVILLA *sanderi* 'Rosea'
Trim before the winter and keep rather dry at 8 °C.

☀ ◌◌ ❀ 5-10 ❄ 5°C

MANDEVILLA *sanderi* 'Scarlet Pimpernel'
Trim somewhat before the winter and keep rather dry at 8 °C.

☀ ◌◌ ❀ 5-10 ❄ 5°C

MANDEVILLA *suaveolens*
Vigorous; cut back to 20 cm above ground-level in autumn and keep rather dry at 5 °C in winter; syn. *M. Laxa*.

☀ ◌◌ ❀ 5-10 ❄ 5°C

MANDEVILLA hybrid

☀ ◌◌ ❀ 5-10 ❄ 5°C

MANDEVILLA large plant

☀️ 〇 ❀ 5-10 ❄️ 8°C

MANETTIA *inflata*
RUBIACEAE
Propagation: by cuttings.
Fertilize weekly; climber; lovely for use in baskets; trim long slender stems; keep rather dry and frost-free in winter; protect from excessive autumn wet; syn. *M. bicolor* and *M. lutea rubra*.

☀️ 〇〇 ❀ 4-6 ❄️ 0°C

MEDICAGO *arborea*
LEGUMINOSAE
Propagation: by seed.
Fertilize regularly; after flowering green, then brown seed pods appear; attractive to butterflies and bees.

☀️ 〇〇 ❀ 4-7 ❄️ 0°C

MEDINELLA *magnifica*
MELASTOMATACEAE
Propagation: by seed or cuttings.
Fertilize regularly; trim after flowering; keep rather dry and frost-free in winter.

☀️ 〇〇 ❀ 4-6 ❄️ 5°C

MELALEUCA *linarifolia*
MYRTACEAE
Propagation: by cuttings.
Needs soft water; water sparingly in winter.

☀️ 〇〇 ❀ 4-7 ❄️ 5°C

MELALEUCA *thymifolia*
MYRTACEAE Propagation: by cuttings.
Fertilize regularly; needs soft water, as with all plants of the *myrte* family; flowers appear on last year's stems, so do not cut back in autumn; winter rather dry and frost-free; can be trained into shape; this must be done after flowering.

☀️ 〇〇 ❀ 7-8 ❄️ -30°C

MENTHA *piperata* 'Eau de Cologne'
LABIATAE/LAMIACEAE
Propagation: by division.
Fertilize weekly; fragrant; invasive; useful when grown in pots because of its scented foliage; hardy.

☀️ 〇〇 ❀ 7-8 ❄️ -25°C

MENTHA *longifolia* 'Buddleia'
LABIATAE/LAMIACEAE
Propagation: by division.
Fertilize weekly; fragrant; invasive; very useful when grown in pots because of its scented foliage; hardy.

☀️ 〇〇 ❀ 6-8 ❄️ 5°C

METROSIDEROS *excelsa*
MYRTACEAE
Propagation: by cuttings.
Fertilize moderately; give soft water; if necessary cut back after flowering – never in autumn; keep rather dry and frost-free in winter; do not let the plant dry out.

☀️ 〇〇 ❀ 6-8 ❄️ 5°C

METROSIDEROS *thomasii*
MYRTACEAE
Propagation: by cuttings.
Fertilize moderately; give soft water; cut back if necessary after flowering – never in autumn; winter rather dry and frost-free; do not let the plant dry out.

☀ ◊◊◊ ❀ 5-10 ❄ -2°C

MILLION BELLS red

☀ ◊◊◊ ❀ 5-10 ❄ -2°C

MILLION BELLS yellow

MILLION BELLS
SOLANACEAE

Propagation: by seed.
A small *surfinia*; very floriferous; easy; fertilize
weekly; difficult to winter; it is better to start each
year with young plants.

☀ ◊◊◊ ❀ 5-10 ❄ -2°C

MILLION BELLS 'Cherry'

☀ ◊◊◊ ❀ 5-10 ❄ -2°C

MILLION BELLS white

☀ ◊◊◊ ❀ 5-10 ❄ -2°C

MILLION BELLS 'Carillon Blue'

☼ ◊◊◊ ❀ 4-10 ❋ 4°C

MIMULUS *aurantiacus* white
SCROPHULARIACEAE
Propagation: by cuttings.
Fertilize weekly; suitable for climbing along wire-netting; also splendid for baskets; trim during growing season to get a second flowering; cut hard back in autumn; winter rather dry and frost-free.

☼ ◊◊◊ ❀ 4-10 ❋ 4°C

MIMULUS *glutinosus* 'Monkey Musk'
SCROPHULARIACEAE
Propagation: by cuttings. Climber; splendid for baskets; fertilize weekly; trim during growing season to induce a second flowering; cut hard back in autumn and keep rather dry and frost-free in winter; syn. *M. glutinosus*.

☼ ◊◊◊ ❀ 4-10 ❋ 4°C

MIMULUS *bifidus* 'Wine'
SCROPHULARIACEAE
Propagation: by cuttings.
Fertilize weekly; climber; also splendid for baskets; vigorous; trim during growing season to induce a second flowering; cut hard back in autumn; keep rather dry and frost-free in winter.

☼ ◊◊◊ ❀ 4-10 ❋ 4°C

MIMULUS 'Strawberry Wine'
SCROPHULARIACEAE
Propagation: by cuttings.
Climber and trailing perennial; vigorous; fertilize weekly; trimming during growing season induces a second flowering; cut hard back in autumn and winter rather dry and frost-free.

☼ ◊◊◊ ❀ 4-10 ❋ 4°C

MIMULUS 'Tangerine'
SCROPHURALIACEAE
See M. 'Strawberry Wine'.

☼ ◊◊◊ ❀ 4-10 ❋ -12°C

MIMULUS white x *aurantiacus*
SCROPHULARIACEAE
See *M*. 'Strawberry Wine'.

☀ ◌◌◌ ✿ 6-9 ❄ 2°C

MIRABILIS *jalapa* yellow
NYCTAGINACEAE
Propagation: divide the rhizome in spring.
Fertilize weekly; dies back in autumn; keep the
rhizomes dry and frost-free; replant in spring.

☀ ◌◌◌ ✿ 6-9 ❄ 2°C

MIRABILIS *jalapa* pink
NYCTAGINACEAE
See *M. jalapa* yellow.

☀ ◌◌◌ ✿ 6-9 ❄ 2°C

MIRABILIS *jalapa* white
NYCTAGINACEAE
See *M. jalapa* yellow.

☀ ◌◌◌ ✿ 6-10 ❄ -3°C

MONOPSIS kapablue
SOLANACEAE
Propagation: by seed or cuttings.
Lovely for baskets; fertilize weekly; wintering is
possible, but it is better to start each year with
young plants; a small kind of petunia.

◐ ◌◌ ✿ 3-10 ❄ 0°C

MURRAYA *paniculata*
RUBIACEAE
Propagation: by cuttings.
Shrub with glossy leaves; evergreen; fragrant;
racemes with orange berries; keep rather dry and
frost-free in winter; syn. *M. exotica.*

◐ ◌◌ ✿ 3-10 ❄ 0°C

MURRAYA *paniculata* berries
RUBIACEAE
Propagation: by cuttings.
Glossy leaves; evergreen; fragrant; racemes with
orange berries; winter rather dry and frost-free.

☀ ◌◌ ✿ 3-6 ❄ 0°C

MUSA *violacea*
MUSACEAE
Fertilize regularly; protect from hot sun; water
moderately during winter.

☀ ◌◌ ✿ 8-9 ❄ 0°C

MUSSAENDRA 'Snowflake'
RUBIACEAE
Propagation: by cuttings.
Fertilize weekly; needs well-drained soil; protect
from hot midday sun; trim after flowering; keep
rather dry and frost-free in winter.

☀ ◌◌◌ ✿ 7-9 ❄ 5°C

MYRTUS *communis*
MYRTACEAE
Propagation: by cuttings.
Needs soft water, as do all plants of the *myrte*
family; fertilize moderately; lovely long-lasting
berries; can be trained into shape; winter rather
dry at 5 ºC.

☀ ◌◌◌ ❀ 7-9 ❄ 5°C

MYRTUS *communis nana*
MYRTACEAE
Propagation: by cuttings.
Needs soft water, as all plants of the *myrte* family; fertilize moderately; can be trained into shape; keep rather dry at 5 °C in winter; a smaller *M. communis.*

☀ ◌◌ ❀ 3-4 ❄ -25°C

NARCISSUS *cyclamineus* 'Tête à Tête'
AMARYLLIDACEAE
Very early-flowering daffodil; splendid for pots and containers.

☀ ◌◌ ❀ 3-4 ❄ -25°C

NARCISSUS *odorus* 'Plenus'
AMARYLLIDACEAE
Fragrant daffodil; splendid for pots in early spring.

☀ ◌◌◌ ❀ 7-9 ❄ 2°C

NEMESIA *strumosa* 'KLM'
SCROPHULARIACEAE
Propagation: by seed.
Sow in spring at 15 °C; needs well-drained soil; fertilize weekly; lovely for pots and baskets.

☀ ◌◌◌ ❀ 7-9 ❄ 2°C

NEMESIA *strumosa* 'Mello Red and White'
SCROPHULARIACEAE
See *N. strumosa* 'KLM'.

☀ ◌◌◌ ❀ 7-9 ❄ 2°C

NEMESIA *strumosa* 'Mello White'
SCROPHULARIACEAE
See *N. strumosa* 'KLM'.

☀ ◌◌◌ ❀ 6-10 ❄ -20°C

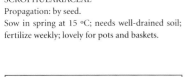

NEPETA *subsessiles*
LABIATAE/LAMIACEAE
Propagation: by division in spring.
Fertilize regularly; needs cool, moist position; upright-grower with bright blue flowers.

☀ ◌◌◌ ❀ 7-10 ❄ 2°C

NICOTIANA *glauca*
SOLANACEAE
Propagation: by cuttings.
Fertilize weekly; scented at night; cut hard back in autumn and keep rather dry and frost-free in winter, if necessary in the dark.

☀ ◌◌◌ ❀ 6-10 ❄ 5°C

NICOTIANA *alata*
SOLANACEAE
Propagation: by seed.
Fertilize weekly; annual *nicotiana* is in all sorts of colours on the market; splendid for containers; named the 'Tobacco plant'.

NERIUM OLEANDER
APOCYNACEAE

Propagation: by cuttings.
Fertilize weekly; needs plenty of water, otherwise the buds will drop out; cut hard back in autumn or spring to keep compact plants; remove withered blooms to prevent diseases; winter rather dry and frost-free; *oleanders* are prone to an unremediable bacterium; cut back attacked plant parts and clean hands and scissors well afterwards; burn down attacked parts.

☀ ◊◊◊ ✿ 6-9 ❄ 4°C

NERIUM OLEANDER hybrid

☀ ◊◊◊ ✿ 6-9 ❄ 4°C

NERIUM OLEANDER hybrid

☀ ◊◊◊ ✿ 6-9 ❄ 4°C

NERIUM OLEANDER hybrid

☀ ◊◊◊ ✿ 6-9 ❄ 4°C

NERIUM OLEANDER hybrid

☀ ◊◊◊ ✿ 6-9 ❄ 4°C

NERIUM OLEANDER hybrid

☼ ◊◊◊ ✿ 6-9   ❄ 4°C

NERIUM OLEANDER hybrid

☼ ◊◊◊ ✿ 6-9   ❄ 4°C

NERIUM OLEANDER hybrid

☼ ◊◊◊ ✿ 6-9   ❄ 4°C

NERIUM OLEANDER hybrid

☼ ◊◊◊ ✿ 6-9   ❄ 4°C

NERIUM OLEANDER hybrid

☼ ◊◊◊ ✿ 6-9   ❄ 4°C

NERIUM OLEANDER 'Album'

☼ ◊◊◊ ✿ 6-9   ❄ 4°C

NERIUM OLEANDER 'Alassio'

☼ ◊◊◊ ✿ 6-9   ❄ 4°C

NERIUM OLEANDER 'Alsace'

☼ ◊◊◊ ✿ 6-9   ❄ 4°C

NERIUM OLEANDER 'Luteum Plenum'

☼ ◊◊◊ ✿ 6-9   ❄ 4°C

NERIUM OLEANDER 'Mont Blanc'

NERIUM OLEANDER 'Petite Red'
Low-growing.

NERIUM OLEANDER 'Petite Salmon'
Low-growing.

NERIUM OLEANDER 'Sealy Pink'

NERIUM OLEANDER *variegata*

NERIUM OLEANDER 'Soleil Levant'

NERIUM OLEANDER 'Ville de la Londe'

☼ ◊◊ ✿ 6-8 ❄ 5°C

NOLANA *paradoxa*
SOLANACEAE
Propagation: by seed.
Fertilize weekly; needs well-drained soil; gives the best results when grown in full sun; pretty annual for baskets and pots.

☼ ◊◊ ✿ 5-10 ❄ 5°C

OCHNA *serrulata*
OCHNACEAE
Propagation: by cuttings.
Fertilize regularly; needs well-drained soil; trim in autumn and water sparingly; winter at 7 °C.

◑ ◊◊ ✿ 4-10 ❄ 0°C

ODONTONEMA *schomburgkianum*
ACANTHACEAE
Propagation: by cuttings.
Fertilize regularly; needs plenty of warmth, moisture and shade in summer; cut back after flowering and fertilize once; winter rather dry at 5 °C; syn. *Thysacanthus rutilans*.

☼ ◊◊ ✿ 4-10 ❄ 0°C

ODONTONEMA *strictum*
ACANTHACEAE
Propagation: by cuttings.
Evergreen shrub; fertilize regularly; needs plenty of warmth, moisture and shade in summer; keep rather dry at 5 °C in winter.

☼ ◊◊ ✿ 6-7 ❄ 0°C

OLEA *europaea*
OLEACEAE
Propagation: by cuttings.
Evergreen shrub with fragrant flowers followed by edible fruit: olives; trim into shape in autumn; keep rather dry and frost-free in winter.

◑ ◊◊ ✿ 5-8 ❄ -15°C

OMPHALODES *cappadocica* 'Starry Eyes'
BORAGINACEAE
Propagation: by division in spring.
Perennial, flowering over a long period; splendid for baskets and containers; fertilize regularly.

☼ ◊◊ ✿ 8-9 ❄ -20°C

OPHIOPOGON *planiscapus* 'Nigrescens'
CONVALLARIACEAE
Propagation: by division.
Clump-forming perennial with almost black leaves; flowers are followed by black berries; when grown in pots, fertilize regularly.

☼ ◊◊ ✿ 7-9 ❄ -5°C

ORIGANUM 'Bristol Cross'
LABIATAE/LAMIACEAE
Propagation: by division.
Pretty perennial, suitable for pots; attractive to bees; fragrant; frost-hardy; it is better to keep rather dry and frost-free in winter.

☼ ◊◊ ✿ 7-9 ❄ -10°C

ORIGANUM 'Pagoda Bells'
LABIATAE/LAMIACEAE
Propagation: by division.
Creeping perennial with long slender stems; lovely for use in baskets because of its pink to mauve abundance of flowers; when grown in pots keep rather dry and frost-free in winter.

☀ ◊◊ ❀ 5-9 ❄ -5°C

OSTEOSPERMUM hybrid
ASTERACEAE/COMPOSITAE
Propagation: by cuttings or seed.
Fertilize weekly; remove withered flowers; start
each year with young plants to get the best results;
lovely for pots.

☀ ◊◊ ❀ 5-9 ❄ -5°C

OSTEOSPERMUM hybrid
ASTERACEAE/COMPOSITAE
See the first *O.* hybrid.

☀ ◊◊ ❀ 5-9 ❄ -5°C

OSTEOSPERMUM hybrid
ASTERACEAE/COMPOSITAE
See the first *O.* hybrid.

☀ ◊◊ ❀ 4-7 ❄ 7°C

OSTEOSPERMUM hybrid
ASTERACEAE/COMPOSITAE
See the first *O.* hybrid.

☀ ◊◊ ❀ 5-9 ❄ -5°C

OSTEOSPERMUM hybrid
ASTERACEAE/COMPOSITAE
See the first *O.* hybrid.

☀ ◊◊ ❀ 5-9 ❄ -5°C

OSTEOSPERMUM *jucundum*
ASTERACEAE/COMPOSITAE
See the first *O.* hybrid.

☀ ◊◊◊ ❀ 4-10 ❄ 5°C

OXALIS
OXALIDACEAE
Propagation: by small bulbs.
Fertilize weekly; pretty for baskets; cut back in
autumn and keep rather dry and frost-free in win-
ter; it is better to start with new bulbs; 'Shamrock'.

☀ ◊◊◊ ❀ 6-10 ❄ 5°C

OXALIS *bowiei*
OXALIDACEAE
Propagation: by small sections of the rhizomes.
Fertilize weekly; pretty in baskets; keep rhizomes
dry and frost-free in winter.

☀ ◊◊◊ ❀ 6-10 ❄ 5°C

OXALIS *hirta*
OXALIDACEAE
Propagation: by small sections of the rhizomes.
Fertilize weekly; pretty for baskets; keep the rhi-
zomes dry and frost-free in winter.

☼ ◌◌ ❀ 5-9 ❄ -5°C

OXALIS *lobata*
OXALIDACEAE
Propagation: by small sections of the rhizomes.
Fertilize weekly; clump-forming perennial; lovely
for baskets and containers; keep the rhizomes dry
and frost-free in winter.

☼ ◌◌◌ ❀ 6-10 ❄ 5°C

OXALIS *obtusa*
OXALIDACEAE
Propagation: by small sections of the rhizomes.
Fertilize weekly; lovely in baskets; keep the rhi-
zomes dry and frost-free.

☼ ◌◌ ❀ 7-9 ❄ 2°C

OXYPETALUM *caeruleum*
ASCLEPIADACEAE
Propagation: by cuttings.
Fertilize weekly; trim somewhat before winter if
necessary; keep rather dry and frost-free in win-
ter; syn. *Tweedia caeruleum*.

☼ ◌◌◌ ❀ 5-7 ❄ 7°C

PACHYSTACHUS *lutea*
ACANTHACEAE
Propagation: by cuttings.
Fertilize weekly; keep rather dry in winter at 8 ºC.

☼ ◌◌ ❀ 7-9 ❄ -15°C

PANDARCAMDA hybrid
IRIDACEAE
Propagation: by division of the rhizomes.
Fertilize weekly; lovely for use in baskets; keep
rather dry in winter; hybrid between 'Belamcanda'
and 'Iris'.

☼ ◌◌ ❀ 7-9 ❄ -15°C

PANDARCAMDA hybrid
IRIDACEAE
See the first *P*. hybrid.

☼ ◌◌ ❀ 7-9 ❄ -15°C

PANDARCAMDA hybrid
See the first *P*. hybrid.

☼ ◌◌ ❀ 7-9 ❄ -15°C

PANDARCAMDA hybrid
IRIDACEAE
See the first *P*. hybrid.

☼ ◌◌◌ ❀ 6-8 ❄ 5°C

PANDOREA *jasminoides*
BIGNONIACEAE
Propagation: by cuttings.
Fertilize weekly; splendid for training along a
wire-netting pillar; trim in autumn and keep
rather dry at 5 ºC in winter; keeps its leaves if
wintered at 10 ºC and with more water.

☀ ◊◊◊ ❀ 6-8 ❄ -8°C

PASSIFLORA *x arisa*
A new hybrid; winter at 10 °C.

☀ ◊◊◊ ❀ 7-10 ❄ 4°C

PASSIFLORA *aurantia*
Very floriferous.

PASSIFLORA
PASSIFLORACEAE

Propagation: by cuttings.
Fertilize weekly; needs some shelter against very hot midday sun; many passifloras produce fruits after flowering; cut hard back in autumn – to 20 cm. above the pot – and keep rather dry in winter; most passifloras winter at 4 °C; otherwise this will be reported under the relevant photo; *P. caerulea* is nearly hardy.

☀ ◊◊◊ ❀ 7-10 ❄ 4°C

PASSIFLORA 'Lavender Lady'
Very floriferous.

☀ ◊◊◊ ❀ 7-10 ❄ 4°C

PASSIFLORA *caerulea*
Fragrant; orange fruits.

☀ ◊◊◊ ❀ 7-10 ❄ 4°C

PASSIFLORA *caerulea x racemosa*

☼ ◊◊◊ ❀ 7-10 ❄ 4°C

PASSIFLORA *cincinnata*
Fragrant; winter at 10 °C.

☼ ◊◊◊ ❀ 7-10 ❄ 4°C

PASSIFLORA *citrina*
Splendid for baskets; winter at 10 °C.

☼ ◊◊◊ ❀ 7-10 ❄ 4°C

PASSIFLORA *edulis* 'Knight'
Winter at 10 °C.

☼ ◊◊◊ ❀ 7-10 ❄ 4°C

PASSIFLORA 'Elizabeth'
Fragrant; floriferous.

☼ ◊◊◊ ❀ 7-10 ❄ 4°C

PASSIFLORA *x exoniensis*
Banana-shaped fruits.

☼ ◊◊◊ ❀ 7-10 ❄ 4°C

PASSIFLORA *herbertiana*
Difficult to make cuttings; it is better to sow; winter at 10 °C; fading flowers; edible fruits.

☼ ◊◊◊ ❀ 7-10 ❄ 4°C

PASSIFLORA *incarnata*
Dies back; frosthardy.

☼ ◊◊◊ ❀ 7-10 ❄ 4°C

PASSIFLORA *incarnata* 'Alba'
A new variety.

☼ ◊◊◊ ❀ 7-10 ❄ 4°C

PASSIFLORA *karwinski*
Fragrant; for baskets.

☀ ◇◇◇ ❀ 7-10   ❄ 4°C

PASSIFLORA 'Kaiserin Eugénie'
Fragrant.

☀ ◇◇◇ ❀ 7-10   ❄ 4°C

PASSIFLORA 'Lavender Lady'
Easy; floriferous.

☀ ◇◇◇ ❀ 7-10   ❄ 4°C

PASSIFLORA *mixta*
Upright flower.

☀ ◇◇◇ ❀ 7-10   ❄ 4°C

PASSIFLORA *morifolia*
Very floriferous.

☀ ◇◇◇ ❀ 7-10   ❄ 4°C

PASSIFLORA *naviculata*

☀ ◇◇◇ ❀ 7-10   ❄ 4°C

PASSIFLORA *peresii*
Winter at 10 ºC.

☀ ◇◇◇ ❀ 7-10   ❄ 4°C

PASSIFLORA *sanguinolenta*
Splendid for baskets; very floriferous.

☀ ◇◇◇ ❀ 7-10   ❄ 4°C

PASSIFLORA 'Sunburst'
Small flower; very floriferous.

☀ ◇◇◇ ❀ 7-10   ❄ 4°C

PASSIFLORA *vitifolia*
Winter at 10 ºC.

☼ ◊◊◊ ❀ 6-8 ❄ 5°C

PANDOREA _jasminoides_ 'Alba'
BIGNONIACEAE
Propagation: by cuttings.
Fertilize weekly; this white variety is an eye-catcher when grown as a pillar; trim in autumn and keep rather dry at 5 °C; keeps its leaves at 10 °C and with more water.

☼ ◊◊◊ ❀ 6-8 ❄ 5°C

PANDOREA _jasminoides_ 'Rosea'
BIGNONIACEAE
Propagation: by cuttings.
Fertilize weekly; a pink variety; climber; trim in autumn and keep rather dry at 5 °C; keeps its leaves at 10 °C and with more water; eye-catcher.

☼ ◊◊◊ ❀ 6-8 ❄ -8°C

PARAHEBE _catarractae_
Propagation: by cuttings.
Fertilize regularly; when grown in pots, protect from severe frost; place in garage or other frost-free room.

◐ ◊◊ ❀ 7-9 ❄ -10°C

PAROCHETUS _communis_
LEGUMINOSAE
Propagation: by division.
Creeping perennial with long slender stems; pretty hanger; short-living; needs renewing regularly; keep young plants in a heated room.

☼ ◊◊ ❀ 7-9 ❄ 5°C

PAVONIA _braziliensis_
MALVACEAE
Propagation: by cuttings.
Fertilize regularly; keep rather dry at 5 °C in winter.

☼ ◊◊ ❀ 7-9 ❄ 5°C

PAVONIA _spinifex_
MALVACEAE
Propagation: by cuttings.
Fertilize regularly; keep rather dry at 5 °C in winter.

☼ ◊◊ ❀ 6-7 ❄ -10°C

PENSTEMON _glabra_
SCROPHULARIACEAE
Propagation: by division.
Fertilize regularly if grown in pots; not very hardy; protect from severe frost with a winter mulch; when grown in pots, protect from frost.

☼ ◊◊ ❀ 6-9 ❄ -10°C

PENSTEMON 'Rich Ruby'
SCROPHULARIACEAE
Propagation: by division.
Fertilize regularly if grown in pots; not very hardy; protect from severe frost with a winter mulch; when grown in pots protect from frost.

◐ ◊◊ ❀ 5-10 ❄ 6°C

PENTAS _lanceolata_ 'Paradise'
RUBIACEAE
Propagation: by cuttings.
Fertilize weekly; easy to grow; flowers throughout the season; if necessary cut back in autumn; if not necessary, keep rather dry and frost-free in winter.

PELARGONIUM *decora* red

PELARGONIUM
GERANIACEAE

Propagation: by cuttings.
Fertilize each 14 days; *pelargoniums* are very nice plants, and flower for months; suitable for many purposes; cut back in autumn and keep rather dry and frost-free in winter; to prevent diseases, mind that the humidity does not becomes too high, especially at a low temperature; if temperature kept at 10 °C plants may flower over winter.

PELARGONIUM 'Ville de Paris'
Abundantly flowering, trailing plant.

PELARGONIUM
Red climber.

PELARGONIUM
Scented foliage.

PELARGONIUM *domesticum*
'Cinderella'

☼ ◊◊ ✽ 5-10 ❄ 5°C

PELARGONIUM *domesticum* 'Doris Hanrock'

☼ ◊◊ ✽ 5-10 ❄ 5°C

PELARGONIUM 'L'Elegante'
Trailing pelargonium with variegated foliage.

☼ ◊◊ ✽ 5-10 ❄ 5°C

PELARGONIUM 'Hills of Snow'
Lovely silver variegated.

☼ ◊◊ ✽ 5-10 ❄ 5°C

PELARGONIUM stellar 'Arctic Star'
Floriferous; resists all kinds of weather.

☼ ◊◊ ✽ 5-10 ❄ 5°C

PELARGONIUM stellar 'Meadowside Midnight'
Floriferous; resists all kinds of weather.

☼ ◊◊ ✽ 5-10 ❄ 5°C

PELARGONIUM 'Mini Czech'
Dwarf with dark leaves.

☀ ◊◊ ✿ 5-10 ❄ 5°C

PELARGONIUM 'Pink Pet'
Strong plant; floriferous.

☀ ◊◊ ✿ 5-10 ❄ 5°C

PELARGONIUM 'Platinum'
Floriferous.

☀ ◊◊ ✿ 5-10 ❄ 5°C

PELARGONIUM 'Robert Fish'
Dwarf with gold variegated foliage.

☀ ◊◊ ✿ 5-10 ❄ 5°C

PELARGONIUM 'Mr. Wren'
Very striking.

☀ ◊◊◊ ✿ 7-10 ❄ 4°C

PELARGONIUM *tricolor*
Hard to winter.

☀ ◊◊ ✿ 5-10 ❄ 5°C

PELARGONIUM
Group.

☀ ◊◊ ✿ 5-10 ❄ 6°C

PENTAS *lanceolata* 'Bright Pink'
RUBIACEAE
See *P. lanceolata* 'Paradise'.

☀ ◊◊ ✿ 5-10 ❄ 6°C

PENTAS *lanceolata* 'Pink'
See *P. lanceolata* 'Paradise'.

◑ ◊◊ ✿ 5-10 ❄ 6°C

PENTAS *lanceolata* 'Candy Stripe'
RUBIACEAE
See *P. lanceolata* 'Paradise'.

☀ ◊◊ ✿ 5-10 ❄ 6°C

PENTAS *lanceolata* 'Royal Red'
RUBIACEAE
See *P. lanceolata* 'Paradise'.

◑ ◊◊ ✿ 5-10 ❄ 6°C

PENTAS *lanceolata* 'Alba'
RUBIACEAE
See *P. lanceolata* 'Paradise'.

☀ ◊◊ ✿ 5-9 ❄ 5°C

PERESKIA *corrilata*
CACTACEAE
Propagation: by cuttings.
Fertilize once a month; pretty climber; keep
rather dry at 5 °C in winter.

☀ ◊◊ ✿ 5-9 ❄ 5°C

PERESKIA *grandiflora*
CACTACEAE
Propagation: by cuttings.
Fertilize once a month; pretty climber; spiny; keep
rather dry at 5 °C.

◑ ◊◊ ✿ 5-10 ❄ 6°C

PERESKIA *sacharosa*
Propagation: by cuttings.
Fertilize once a month; pretty plant for containers; spiny; keep rather dry at 5 °C in winter; syn. *P.
nemorosa*.

◑ ◊◊ ✿ 5-7 ❄ -25°C

PERNETTYA *mucronata* 'Lilacina'
ERICACEAE
Propagation: by cuttings.
Fertilize regularly if grown in pots; needs somewhat acidic soil; flowers are followed by berries;
grow male and female plants together to get
berries.

☼◑ ◊◊ ❀5-7 ❄-25°C

PERNETTYA *mucronata* 'Alba'
ERICACEAE
Propagation: by cuttings.
Fertilize regularly if grown in pots; needs somewhat acidic soil; flowers are followed by berries;
grow male and female plants together to get
berries.

☼ ◊◊◊ ❀3-8 ❄8°C

PETREA *volubilis*
VERBENACEAE
Propagation: by cuttings.
Fertilize regularly; particular climber with rough
leaves; cut back long slender stems in autumn and
keep rather dry and frost-free in winter.

☼ ◊◊◊ ❀5-10 ❄0°C

PETUNIA double white
SOLANACEAE
Propagation: by seed.
Fertilize weekly; long slender stems could be
trimmed; not recommended for wintering; it is
better to start each year with young plants.

☼ ◊◊◊ ❀5-10 ❄0°C

PETUNIA 'Strawberry Sunday'
SOLANACEAE
See *P*. double white.

☼ ◊◊◊ ❀5-10 ❄0°C

PETUNIA
SOLANACEAE
See *P*. double white.

☼ ◊◊◊ ❀6-12 ❄10°C

PHASAEOLUS *caracalla*
LEGUMINOSAE
Propagation: by seed.
Fertilize weekly; vigorous climber; striking; can
flower also in winter at 15 ºC; trim slender stems
in spring.

☼ ◊◊◊ ❀6-7 ❄-15°C

PHLOMIS *fruticosa*
LABIATAE/LAMIACEAE
Propagation: by division or cuttings.
Fertilize regularly; not very hardy perennial;
splendid in pots in a yellow corner.

☼ ◊◊ ❀5-6 ❄-25°C

PHLOX *bifida*
POLEMONIACEAE
Propagation: by division.
Clump-forming evergreen perennial; suitable
for pots.

☼ ◊◊ ❀n.v.t. ❄10°C

PHOENIX *canariensis*
ARECACEAE/PALMAE
Fertilize once a month; in autumn, beautiful
orange fruits appear in large racemes; water
sparingly in winter.

☼ ◌◌ ❀ n.v.t. ❄ 10°C

PHOENIX **canariensis** dades
ARECACEAE/PALMAE
Fertilize once a month; in autumn, beautiful orange fruits appear in large racemes; water sparingly in winter.

☼ ◌◌◌ ❀ 6-11 ❄ 4°C

PHYGELIUS **aqualis** 'Yellow Trumpet'
SCROPHULARIACEAE
Propagation: by cuttings.
Fertilize weekly; wrongly named the 'yellow fuchsia'; cut hard back in autumn; keep rather dry and frost-free in winter.

☼ ◌◌◌ ❀ 6-11 ❄ 4°C

PHYGELIUS **capensis** 'Trewidden'
SCROPHULARIACEAE
Propagation: by cuttings.
Fertilize weekly; cut hard back in autumn and keep rather dry and frost-free in winter; P. capensis is more trailing than P. aqualis.

☼ ◌◌ ❀ 5-6 ❄ 0°C

PHYLICA **ericoides**
RHAMNACEAE
Propagation: by cuttings.
Fertilize regularly; needs humus-rich, well-drained soil; winter rather dry.

☼◐ ◌◌ ❀ 2-5 ❄ -20°C

PIERIS **japonica** 'Valley Valentine'
ERICACEAE
Propagation: by cuttings.
Fertilize regularly if grown in pots; recommended for growing in containers because of its early flowering; splendid racemes with dark-red flowers; tolerates shade.

☼ ◌◌ ❀ n.v.t. ❄ -25°C

PINUS **nigra** 'Pierrick Bregum'
PINACEAE
Slow-growing; fragrant; recommended for pots on a terrace.

☼ ◌◌ ❀ 4-6 ❄ -5°C

PITTOSPORUM **tenuifolium** 'Tom Thumb'
PITTOSPORACEAE
Propagation: by cuttings.
Fertilize regularly; low-growing shrub; fragrant; pretty, bronze-coloured foliage; when grown in pots, keep rather dry and frost-free in winter.

☼ ◌◌ ❀ 5-7 ❄ -5°C

PITTOSPORUM **tobira**
PITTOSPORACEAE
Propagation: by cuttings.
Fertilize regularly; scented flowers followed by yellow-brown seed pods; grown in pots: keep rather dry and frost-free in winter; could be trimmed if necessary.

☼ ◌◌ ❀ 5-7 ❄ -5°C

PITTOSPORUM **tobira** berries
PITTOSPORACEAE
See P. tobira.

☀ ◌◌ ❀ 5-7 ❄ -5°C

PITTOSPORUM *tobira variegata*
PITTOSPORACEAE
Propagation: by cuttings.
See *P. tobira*.

☀ ◌◌◌ ❀ 5-11 ❄ 4°C

PLUMBAGO *auriculata*
PLUMBAGINACEAE
Propagation: by cuttings.
Fertilize weekly; lovely climber; cut hard back in
autumn; winter rather dry and frost-free; named
'Leadwort'; syn. *P. capensis*.

☀ ◌◌◌ ❀ 5-11 ❄ 4°C

PLUMBAGO *auricula alba*
PLUMBAGINACEAE
Propagation: by cuttings.
Fertilize weekly; lovely climber; splendid when
grown as a pillar; cut hard back in autumn; winter
rather dry and frost-free; syn. *P. capensis*.

☀ ◌◌ ❀ 12-1 ❄ 10°C

PLUMBAGO *indica*
PLUMBAGINACEAE
Propagation: by cuttings.
Hard to grow; winter flowering; needs to winter at
a minimum of 14 ºC.

☀ ◌◌ ❀ 7-9 ❄ 8°C

PLUMERIA *rubra var. acutifolia*
APOCYNACEAE
Propagation: by cuttings.
Fertilize regularly; keep almost dry during winter,
at 10 ºC.

☀ ◌◌◌ ❀ 7-11 ❄ 5°C

PODRANEA *brysei*
BIGNONIACEAE
Propagation: by cuttings.
Fertilize weekly; pretty climber; cut hard back in
autumn and keep rather dry and frost-free in
winter.

☀ ◌◌◌ ❀ 7-11 ❄ 5°C

PODRANEA *ricasoliana*
BIGNONIACEAE
Propagation: by cuttings.
Fertilize weekly; climber; cut hard back in
autumn; winter rather dry and frost-free.

☀ ◌◌ ❀ 6-10 ❄ 6°C

POLYGALA *dalmaciana*
POLYGALACEAE
Propagation: by cuttings.
Fertilize weekly; flowers at intervals; needs well-
drained soil; trim into shape after flowering; winter rather dry at 7 ºC; syn. *P. myrtifolia* var.
grandiflora.

☀ ◌ ❀ 6-10 ❄ 0°C

POLYGALA *fruticosa*
POLYGALACEAE
Propagation: by cuttings.
Fertilize regularly; needs well-drained soil; dis-
likes "wet feet"; trim after flowering; keep rather
dry and frost-free in winter.

☼ ◊◊◊ ❀ 6-11   ❄ 10°C

PORTULACA ***umbratiolo***
PORTULACACEAE
Propagation: by seed.
Fertilize weekly; with its bright colours, splendid
for baskets or in a bowl at the table; at drought, the
leaves fold up.

☼ ◊◊◊ ❀ 6-11   ❄ 10°C

PORTULACA ***umbratiolo***
PORTULACACEAE
See the first *P. umbratiolo.*

☼ ◊◊◊ ❀ 6-11   ❄ 10°C

PORTULACA ***umbratiolo***
PORTULACACEAE
See the first *P. umbratiolo.*

☼ ◊◊◊ ❀ 6-11   ❄ 10°C

PORTULACA ***umbratiolo***
PORTULACACEAE
See the first *P. umbratiolo.*

☼ ◊◊◊ ❀ 6-11   ❄ 10°C

PORTULACA ***umbratiolo***
PORTULACACEAE
See the first *P. umbratiolo.*

☼ ◊◊◊ ❀ 6-11   ❄ 10°C

PORTULACA ***umbratiolo***
PORTULACACEAE
See the first *P. umbratiolo.*

☼ ◊◊ ❀ 6-10 ❄ 5°C

POLYGALA *myrtifolia*
POLYGALACEAE
Propagation: by cuttings.
Fertilize weekly; needs well-drained soil; flowers at
intervals; trim after flowering; keep rather dry and
frost-free in winter.

☼ ◊◊ ❀ 6-8 ❄ -10°C

POLYGONUM *capitatum*
POLYGONACEAE
Propagation: by division.
Invasive perennial; suitable for pots; not really
hardy; protect from severe frost with a winter
mulch; if grown in pots, keep frost-free in winter.

☼ ◊◊ ❀ 5-6 ❄ -20°C

PONCIRUS *trifoliata*
RUTACEAE
Propagation: by seed or cuttings.
Fertilize regularly; has very sharp spines; after
flowering, green fruits appear.

☼ ◊◊ ❀ 3-4 ❄ -20°C

PRIMULA *x pubescens*
PRIMULACEAE
Propagation: by division.
Fertilize regularly; because of its early flowering,
splendid for pots on a terrace.

☼ ◊◊ ❀ 3-4 ❄ -20°C

PRIMULA *x pubescens*
PRIMULACEAE
See the first *P. x pubescens*.

☼ ◊◊ ❀ 3-4 ❄ -25°C

PRIMULA *vulgaris* 'Double White'
PRIMULACEAE
See the first *P. x pubescens*.

☼ ◊◊ ❀ 3-4 ❄ -25°C

PRIMULA *vulgaris subsp. sibthorpii*
PRIMULACEAE
Propagation: by division.
Fertilize regularly; because of it early flowering
splendid for pots on a terrace; eye-catcher.

☼ ◊◊ ❀ 3-4 ❄ -10°C

PRIMULA
PRIMULACEAE
See the first *P. x pubescens*.

☼ ◊◊◊ ❀ 3-4 ❄ -10°C

PRIMULA
PRIMULACEAE
See the first *P. x pubescens*.

☼ ◊◊◊ ❀ 6-7 ❄ -8°C

PROSTANTHERA *cuneata*
LABIATAE/LAMIACEAE
Propagation: by cuttings.
Fertilize regularly; crushed leaves are strongly aromatic; trim after flowering, but not too short; keep rather dry and frost-free in winter.

☼ ◊◊◊ ❀ 6-8 ❄ -3°C

PROSTANTHERA *lasianthus*
LABIATAE/LAMIACEAE
Propagation: by cuttings.
Fertilize regularly; needs well-drained, moist soil; trim a bit in autumn; keep rather dry and frost-free.

☼ ◊◊◊ ❀ 6-8 ❄ 0°C

PROSTANTHERA 'Poorinda Ballerina'
LABIATAE/LAMIACEAE
Propagation: by cuttings.
Fertilize regularly; needs moist, well-drained soil; trim in autumn, but not too short; keep rather dry and frost-free in winter; a hybrid from Australia.

☼ ◊◊ ❀ 8-9 ❄ 0°C

PSEUDOCALYNUM *alliacum*
Little is known about this plant.

☼ ◊◊◊ ❀ 4-5 ❄ 4°C

PSIDIUM *guajava*
MYRTACEAE
Fertilize weekly; fragrant; after flowering the vitamin C-rich guava fruits appear; keep rather dry and frost-free in winter; could be trained into shape.

☼ ◊◊ ❀ 3-5 ❄ -25°C

PULMONARIA *saccharata*
BORAGINACEAE
Propagation: by division.
Hardy perennial; because of its early flowering, splendid for pots on a terrace.

☼ ◊◊◊ ❀ 6-7 ❄ 4°C

PUNICA *granatum*
PUNICACEAE
Propagation: by cuttings.
Fertilize weekly; after mid-July, give less water and fertilizer; after flowering the decorative pomegranates appear; cut back in autumn and keep rather dry and frost-free in winter.

☼ ◊◊◊ ❀ 6-7 ❄ 4°C

PUNICA *granatum* pomegranates
PUNICACEAE
Propagation: by cuttings.
See *P. granatum*

☼ ◊◊◊ ❀ 6-7 ❄ 4°C

PUNICA *granatum flore plena*
PUNICACEAE
See *P. granatum*.

☀ ◊◊◊ ✿ 6-9 ❄ 0°C

QUAMOCLIT *pennata*
CONVOLVULACEAE
Propagation: by seed.
Fertilize weekly; pretty, annual climber with striking red flowers; syn. *Ipomoea quamoclit*.

☀ ◊◊◊ ✿ 6-9 ❄ 0°C

QUAMOCLIT *pennata* orange
CONVOLVULACEAE
Propagation: by seed.
Fertilize weekly; pretty, annual climber with striking orange flowers; syn. *Ipomoea quamoclit*.

☀ ◊◊◊ ✿ 7-9 ❄ 10°C

QUISQUALIS *indica* young flower
COMBRETACEAE
Propagation: by cuttings.
Fertilize regularly; in a few days flowers change from white to pink to red; fragrant; keep rather dry and frost-free in winter.

☀ ◊◊◊ ✿ 7-9 ❄ 10°C

QUISQUALIS *indica* flowers after 2 days
COMBRETACEAE
See *Q. indica* young flower.

☀ ◊◊◊ ✿ 7-9 ❄ 10°C

QUISQUALIS *indica* adult
COMBRETACEAE
See *Q. indica* young flower.

☀ ◊◊◊ ✿ 5-8 ❄ 0°C

RANUNCULUS
RANUNCULACEAE
Propagation: by seed.
Striking annual, early flowering; recommended for terrace pots.

☀ ◊◊◊ ✿ 5-8 ❄ 0°C

RANUNCULUS
RANUNCULACEAE
See first *Ranunculus*.

☀ ◊◊◊ ✿ 5-8 ❄ 0°C

RANUNCULUS
RANUNCULACEAE
See first *Ranunculus*.

☀ ◊◊◊ ✿ 2-10 ❄ 7°C

REINWARDTIA *indica*
LINACEAE
Propagation: by cuttings.
Fertilize regularly; with a minimum temperature of 13 °C this plant could flower in winter; after flowering, water less.

☀ ◊◊ ❀ 7 ❄ 10°C

RHAPIS *excelsea*
ARECACEAE/PALMAE
Propagation: by division.
Fertilize regularly; needs moist, well-drained soil;
water less during winter.

☀ ◊◊◊ ❀ 6-11 ❄ 6°C

RHODOCHITON *atrosanguineus*
SCROPHULARIACEAE
Propagation: by seed.
Fertilize weekly; climber; cut hard back in autumn
and keep rather dry and frost-free; hard to winter;
mostly grown as annual; also recommended as
trailing plant.

☀ ◊◊◊ ❀ 3-4 ❄ -25°C

RHODODENDRON *praecox*
ERICACEAE
Lovely, early-flowering hardy shrub; late night-
frost could damage the early flowers.

☀ ◊◊◊ ❀ 6-9 ❄ 0°C

RICINUS *communis*
EUPHORBIACEAE
Propagation: by seed
Fertilize regularly; before sowing, soak seed for 24
hours; plant out when danger of frost has passed;
mostly grown as annual; 'Castor oil plant'.

☀ ◊◊◊ ❀ 6-7 ❄ 8°C

RONDELETIA *splendens*
RUBIACEAE
Propagation: by cuttings.
Fertilize weekly; pretty summer-flowering shrub;
cut back in autumn and keep rather dry at 7 °C in
winter.

☀ ◊◊ ❀ 6-8 ❄ 10°C

RUELLIA *brittonianum* 'Blue'
ACANTHACEAE
Propagation: by cuttings.
Fertilize weekly; prone to wind; could be trimmed
into shape; winter at 15 °C.

☀ ◊◊ ❀ 6-8 ❄ 10°C

RUELLIA *brittonianum* 'White'
ACANTHACEAE
See *R. brittonianum* 'Blue'.

☀ ◊◊ ❀ 6-8 ❄ 10°C

RUELLIA *brittonianum* 'Pink'
ACANTHACEAE
See *R. brittonianum* 'Blue'.

☀ ◊◊ ❀ 6-8 ❄ 10°C

RUELLIA *mackoyana*
ACANTHACEAE
Propagation: by cuttings.
Fertilize weekly; creeping shrub; splendid for
baskets; winter at 15 °C; water less.

☀   ◊◊   ✿ 4-6   ❄ -5°C

ROSMARINUS *lavendulaceus*
Creeping; not hardy.

☀   ◊◊   ✿ 4-6   ❄ -5°C

ROSMARINUS *officinalis* 'Boule'
Creeping cultivar.

ROSMARINUS
LABIATAE/LAMIACEAE

Propagation: by cuttings.
Fragrant; needs poor soil and moderate fertilizer;
half-hardy; keep rather dry and frost-free in winter for the best results; creeping cultivars are
splendid for use in baskets.

☀   ◊◊   ✿ 4-6   ❄ -5°C

ROSMARINUS *officinalis* 'Corsican
Blue'
Creeping cultivar.

☀   ◊◊   ✿ 4-6   ❄ -5°C

ROSMARINUS *officinalis* hybrid
Vigorous *rosmarinus*.

☀   ◊◊   ✿ 4-6   ❄ -5°C

ROSMARINUS *officinalis* hybrid
Pretty cultivar.

☼ ◊◊ ✿ 4-6 ❄ -5°C

ROSMARINUS *officinalis* 'Majorica Pink'
Pink variety.

☼ ◊◊ ✿ 4-6 ❄ -5°C

ROSMARINUS *officinalis* 'Sissinghurst White'
The white rosmary.

☼ ◊◊ ✿ 4-6 ❄ -5°C

ROSMARINUS *officinalis* 'Vicomte de Noai'
Creeping.

☼ ◊◊ ✿ 4-6 ❄ -5°C

ROSMARINUS 'Pyramidalis'
Vigorous, upright-growing variety.

☼ ◊◊ ✿ 4-6 ❄ -5°C

☼ ◊◊ ✿ 4-6 ❄ -5°C

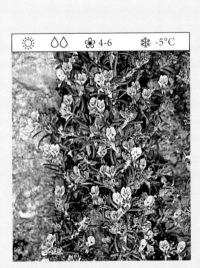

ROSMARINUS

ROSMARINUS

☀ ◊◊ ✿ 6-8 ❄ 10°C

RUELLIA 'Shooting Star'
ACANTHACEAE
Propagation: by cuttings.
Fertilize weekly; could be trimmed into shape;
winter at 15 ºC; water less.

☀ ◊◊◊ ✿ 6-9 ❄ 10°C

RUSSELIA *equisetiformis* 'Alba'
SCROPHULARIACEAE
Propagation: by cuttings.
Fertilize weekly; striking, trailing perennial; needs
plenty of water in summer; cut back old stems in
autumn and keep rather dry at 10 ºC in winter; not
easy.

☀ ◊◊◊ ✿ 6-9 ❄ 10°C

RUSSELIA *equisetiformis*
SCROPHULARIACEAE
Propagation: by cuttings.
Fertilize weekly; striking, trailing perennial; needs
plenty of water in summer; cut back old stems in
autumn; keep rather dry at 10 ºC in winter; not
easy.

☀ ◊◊◊ ✿ 6-11 ❄ 10°C

RUTTHYA *fruticosa*
ACANTHACEAE
Propagation: by cuttings.
Fertilize weekly; long slender stems could be
trimmed; cut hard back in autumn; keep rather
dry at 10 ºC in winter; striking flower.

☀ ◊◊◊ ✿ 6-10 ❄ 10°C

☀ ◊◊◊ ✿ 6-11 ❄ 10°C

RUTTHYA *fruticosa* 'Scholesei'
ACANTHACEAE
Propagation: by cuttings.
Fertilize weekly; long slender stems could be
trimmed; cut hard back in autumn and keep
rather dry at 10 ºC in winter; striking flower.

RUTTHYA *ruspolia*
ACANTHACEAE
Propagation: by cuttings.
Fertilize weekly; cut hard back in autumn; keep rather dry at 10 ºC in winter.

☀ ◊◊◊ ❀ 7-10 ❄ 5°C

SALVIA *canariensis*

☀ ◊◊◊ ❀ 7-10 ❄ 5°C

SALVIA *chamaedryoides*

SALVIA
LABIATAE/LAMIACEAE

Propagation: by cuttings.
Fertilize weekly; many cultivars are perennials
and suitable for growing in containers; many
varieties have scented foliage; cut hard back in
autumn and keep rather dry and frost-free in
winter; easy to grow.

☀ ◊◊◊ ❀ 7-10 ❄ 5°C

SALVIA *atrocyanea*
Dies back above ground.

☀ ◊◊◊ ❀ 7-10 ❄ 5°C

SALVIA *chappelensis*
Continuously flowering.

☀ ◊◊◊ ❀ 7-10 ❄ 5°C

SALVIA *cinnebarina*

☼ ◊◊◊ ✿ 7-10 ❄ 5°C

SALVIA ***coccinea*** 'Pink and White'
Two-coloured flowers.

☼ ◊◊◊ ✿ 7-10 ❄ 5°C

SALVIA ***discolor***
Uncommon, coloured flower.

☼ ◊◊◊ ✿ 7-10 ❄ 5°C

SALVIA ***elegans***
Floriferous.

☼ ◊◊◊ ✿ 7-10 ❄ 5°C

SALVIA ***farinacea***
Mostly grown as annual.

☼ ◊◊◊ ✿ 7-10 ❄ 5°C

SALVIA ***farinaceae*** light form

☼ ◊◊◊ ✿ 7-10 ❄ 5°C

SALVIA ***fulgens***

☼ ◊◊◊ ✿ 7-10 ❄ 5°C

SALVIA ***gregii*** 'Alba'
Floriferous.

☼ ◊◊◊ ✿ 7-10 ❄ 5°C

SALVIA ***guarantica*** 'Blue Enigma'
Lovely, flowered spikes.

☼ ◊◊◊ ✿ 7-10 ❄ 5°C

SALVIA ***guarantica*** 'Dark Skies'

☼　◊◊◊　❁ 7-10　❄ 5°C

SALVIA *involucrata*

☼　◊◊◊　❁ 7-10　❄ 5°C

SALVIA *jamensis* 'Pat Vlasto'
Special colour.

☼　◊◊◊　❁ 7-10　❄ 5°C

SALVIA *leucantha*

☼　◊◊◊　❁ 7-10　❄ 5°C

SALVIA *microphylla*
Pretty, leathery leaves.

☼　◊◊◊　❁ 7-10　❄ 5°C

SALVIA *officinalis tricolor*

☼　◊◊◊　❁ 7-10　❄ 5°C

SALVIA *patens*

☼　◊◊◊　❁ 7-10　❄ 5°C

SALVIA *patens* 'Cambridge Blue'

☼　◊◊◊　❁ 7-10　❄ 5°C

SALVIA *patens* 'White Trophy'

☼　◊◊◊　❁ 7-10　❄ 5°C

SALVIA *pitcherii* 'Azura'

☼ ◊◊◊ ❀ 7-10 ❄ 5°C

SALVIA *regla*

☼ ◊◊◊ ❀ 7-10 ❄ 5°C

SALVIA *repens*
Strong, aromatic foliage.

☼ ◊◊◊ ❀ 7-10 ❄ 5°C

SALVIA *splendens* purple
Mostly grown as annual.

☼ ◊◊◊ ❀ 7-10 ❄ 5°C

SALVIA *splendens* pink
Mostly grown as annual.

☼ ◊◊◊ ❀ 7-10 ❄ 5°C

SALVIA *splendens* red
Mostly grown as annual.

☼ ◊◊◊ ❀ 7-10 ❄ 5°C

SALVIA red

☀ ◊◊◊ ✿ 6-10 ❄ -5°C

SANVITALIA *procumbens*
ASTERACEAE/COMPOSITAE
Propagation: by seed.
Fertilize weekly; creeping annual; suitable for baskets and containers.

☀ ◊◊ ✿ 1-3 ❄ -20°C

SARCOCOCCA *confusa*
BUXACEAE
Propagation: by cuttings.
Grows only in sun if soil remains sufficiently moist; fertilize regularly; fragrant; after flowering, glossy black berries appear; very suitable for pots because of its winter flowering.

◑ ◊◊ ✿ 1-3 ❄ -5°C

SARCOCOCCA *ruscifolia*
BUXACEAE
Propagation: by cuttings.
Scented flowers appear in winter, followed by dark red berries; very suitable for use in pots because of its winter flowering.

☀ ◊◊◊ ✿ 4-6 ❄ 0°C

SCADOXUS *multifloris*
AMARYLLIDACEAE
Propagation: by seed or dividing the bulbs.
Bulbous perennial; fertilize regularly; dies back after flowering; keep the bulb dry in winter and replant in spring.

☀ ◊◊◊ ✿ 4-11 ❄ 2°C

SCAEVOLA *aemula* 'Alba'
GOODENIACEAE
Propagation: by cuttings.
Fertilize weekly; could be trimmed regularly; cut hard back in autumn; keep rather dry and frost-free; often disappointing; it is better to start each year with young plants.

☀ ◊◊◊ ✿ 4-11 ❄ 2°C

SCAEVOLA *aemula* 'Blue Fan'
GOODENIACEAE
Propagation: by seed or cuttings.
Fertilize weekly; could be trimmed regularly; cut hard back in autumn; keep rather dry and frost-free in winter; often disappointing; it is better to start each year with young plants.

◑ ◊◊ ✿ 3-5 ❄ 5°C

SCHAUERIA *calicotricha*
ACANTHACEAE
Propagation: by cuttings.
Fertilize regularly; needs well-drained soil; winter rather dry at 5 °C.

☀ ◊◊ ✿ 6-7 ❄ 10°C

SCHEFFLERA *venulosa*
ARALIACEAE
Propagation: by cuttings.
Fertilize regularly; water less in winter and keep at 10 °C.

◑ ◊◊ ✿ 6-8 ❄ -25°C

SCUTELLARIA *costaricana*
LABIATAE/LAMIACEAE
Propagation: by division.
Clump-forming, spreading perennial; very suitable for pots because of its low growth.

☀ ◊◊ ❀ 9-10 ❄ -25°C

SEDUM *spectabile*
CRASSULACEAE
Propagation: by division.
Stately perennial, 40 cm. high; because of its late
flowers, very suitable for pots on a terrace.

☀ ◊◊◊ ❀ 6-10 ❄ 7°C

SENECIO *confusus* large
ASTERACEAE/COMPOSITAE
Propagation: by cuttings.
Vigorous climber; makes long slender stems; fertilize weekly; cut hard back in autumn and keep
rather dry at 10 °C in winter; water more if leaves
appear.

☀ ◊◊◊ ❀ 6-10 ❄ 7°C

SENECIO *confusus* small
ASTERACEAE/COMPOSITAE
Propagation: by cuttings.
Vigorous climber; fertilize weekly; blooms more
than *S. confusus* large; cut hard back in autumn
and keep rather dry at 10 °C during winter; water
more if leaves appear.

☀ ◊◊ ❀ 6-8 ❄ 7°C

SENECIO *heritieri*
ASTERACEAE/COMPOSITAE
Propagation: by cuttings.
Fertilize regularly; fragrant racemes with flowers;
cut back in autumn and keep rather dry at 5 °C in
winter; syn. *Pericallis lanata*.

☀ ◊◊ ❀ 3-4 ❄ -25°C

SKIMMIA *laureola* 'Kew White'
RUTACEAE
Propagation: by cuttings.
Fertilize regularly if grown in pots; evergreen; after
flowering, splendid white berries appear; recom-
mended for pots; keep on a terrace during winter.

☀ ◊◊ ❀ 3-4 ❄ -25°C

SKIMMIA *reevesiana*
RUTACEAE
See *S. laureola* 'Kew White'.

☀ ◊◊ ❀ 9-12 ❄ -25°C

SKIMMIA *japonica* 'Rubella'
RUTACEAE
See *S. laureola* 'Kew White'.

☀ ◊◊◊ ❀ 7-8 ❄ 5°C

SOLANDRA *maxima*
SOLANACEAE
Propagation: by cuttings.
Fertilize regularly; fragrant climber; trim long
slender stems; winter rather dry at 5 °C.

☀ ◊◊◊ ❀ 4-11 ❄ 6°C

SOLLYA *heterophylla*
PITTOSPORACEAE
Propagation: by cuttings.
Fertilize weekly; keep rather dry at 8 °C in winter;
trim old stems in spring; there are also white and
pink varieties on the market.

☼ ◊◊◊ ✿ 6-11 ❄ 5°C

SOLANUM *atropurpureum*

☼ ◊◊◊ ✿ 6-11 ❄ 5°C

SOLANUM *aviculare*
The Aboriginals eat the fruit because of its
vitamin C.

SOLANUM
SOLANACEAE

Propagation: by cuttings.
All *Solanums* need a fertilizer weekly; almost all of
them are vigorous climbers; trim long slender
stems during growing season; cut hard back in
autumn and keep rather dry and frost-free in
winter, if necessary in dark – they then lose their
leaves; many produce edible fruits.

☼ ◊◊◊ ✿ 6-11 ❄ -12°C

SOLANUM *bonariense*
Continuously flowering.

☼ ◊◊◊ ✿ 6-11 ❄ 5°C

SOLANUM *crispum* 'Glasnevin'
Suitable for baskets.

☼ ◊◊◊ ✿ 6-11 ❄ 5°C

SOLANUM *jasminoides*
Survives outdoors during not too severe winters.

☼ ◊◊◊ ✤ 6-11 ❄ 5°C

SOLANUM *jasminoides*
Pretty climber.

☼ ◊◊◊ ✤ 6-11 ❄ 5°C

SOLANUM *jasminoides variegata*
A variegatied variety.

☼ ◊◊◊ ✤ 6-11 ❄ 5°C

SOLANUM *mammosum* fruits
Very unusual fruits.

☼ ◊◊◊ ✤ 6-11 ❄ 5°C

SOLANUM *muricatum*
Shrub with arching stems.

☼ ◊◊◊ ✤ 6-11 ❄ 5°C

SOLANUM *muricatum* fruits
Delicious sweet fruits.

☼ ◊◊◊ ✤ 6-11 ❄ 5°C

SOLANUM *piricante*
Spiny.

☼ ◊◊◊ ✤ 6-11 ❄ 5°C

SOLANUM *quioense*
Spiny; orange edible fruits; flowers appear near
the stem.

☼ ◊◊◊ ✤ 6-11 ❄ 5°C

SOLANUM *rantonnettii*
Could be grown as shrub or climber.

☼ ◊◊◊ ✤ 6-11 ❄ 5°C

SOLANUM *rantonnettii* 'Outre Mer'
Very dark blue variety.

Some *Solanums* have spikes: *S. wendlandii*, for instance, can be pretty mean; this you usually only notice after you've been pricked; *S. piricante* and *S. quioense* are also spiky; *S. aviculare* grows edible fruit after flowering – it can easily survive winter but often you'll also find young plants in the vicinity of the old; *S. muricatum* has deliciously sweet, lilac-crème coloured fruit; *S. jasminoides* is beautiful when trained along a wire-netting pillar, and young plants in a basket (if watered, fertilized and cut back regularly) can quickly grow into a lovely, attractive hanging plant.

☼   ◊◊◊   ❀ 6-11   ❄ 5°C

SOLANUM *rantonnettii* 'Royal Robe'
Dark blue variety.

☼   ◊◊◊   ❀ 6-11   ❄ 5°C

SOLANUM *rantonnettii variegata*
Variegated variety.

☼   ◊◊◊   ❀ 6-11   ❄ 5°C

SOLANUM *sysibrifolium*

☼   ◊◊◊   ❀ 6-11   ❄ 5°C

☼   ◊◊◊   ❀ 6-11   ❄ 5°C

SOLANUM *wendlandii*
Splendid spiny climber.

SOLANUM *wendlandii*
Trim long slender stems during growing season; very spiny.

☀ ◊◊◊ ❀ 3-4 ❄ 6°C

SPARMANNIA *africana*
TILIACEAE
Propagation: by cuttings.
Fertilize weekly; vigorous plant that needs plenty of fertilizer; cut hard back in autumn and keep rather dry at 6 °C in winter; 'African Hemp'.

☀ ◊◊ ❀ 6-9 ❄ -8°C

SPARTIUM *junceum*
LEGUMINOSAE
Propagation: by cuttings.
Fertilize regularly; frost-tender shrub with arching branches; abundant flowering; winter rather dry and frost-free; if necessary, trim in spring.

☀ ◊◊ ❀ 7-10 ❄ -10°C

SPHAERALCEA *munroana compacta*
MALVACEAE
Propagation: by cuttings.
Fertilize weekly; grows well in baskets; trim in autumn and keep rather dry and frost-free in winter.

☀ ◊◊◊ ❀ 5-9 ❄ 10°C

STEPHANOTIS *floribunda*
ASCLEPIADACEAE
Propagation: by cuttings.
Fertilize regularly; keep rather dry in winter; give no fertilizer.

☀ ◊◊◊ ❀ 5-9 ❄ 10°C

STEPHANOTIS *floribunda* variegata
ASCLEPIADACEAE
Propagation: by cuttings.
Fertilize regularly; winter rather dry; give no fertilizer; variegated hybrid.

☀ ◊◊ ❀ 5-7 ❄ 5°C

STRELITZIA *reginae*
MUSACEAE
Propagation: by cuttings.
Fertilize regularly; needs a warm place; keep rather dry in winter; needs a cool place; the buds are born during this cool period; give a warmer place after that and water more.

☀ ◊◊◊ ❀ 4-11 ❄ 10°C

STREPTOCARPUS *saxorum*
GESNERIACEAE
Propagation: by cuttings.
Fertilize weekly; suitable for baskets; keep rather dry at 10 °C in winter; from experience it is known that September cuttings produce better bloom the next year.

☀ ◊◊◊ ❀ 4-8 ❄ 5°C

STREPTOSOLEN *jamesonii* orange
SOLANACEAE
Propagation: by cuttings.
Fertilize weekly; semi-climber; best grown with sufficient difference between day and night temperatures in spring; cut back in autumn; keep rather dry in winter.

☀ ◊◊◊ ❀ 4-8 ❄ 5°C

STREPTOSOLEN *jamesonii* yellow
SOLANACEAE
Propagation: by cuttings.
Fertilize weekly; semi-climber; best grown with sufficient difference between day and night temperature in spring; cut back in autumn and keep rather dry in winter.

☼ ◊◊◊ ✽ 5-11   ❄ 5°C

SURFINIA *rose pink*

☼ ◊◊◊ ✽ 5-11   ❄ 5°C

SURFINIA *hot pink*
SOLANACEAE
See *S.* rose pink.

SURFINIA
SOLANACEAE

Fertilize weekly; grows well everywhere; trim long slender stems; wintering is possible but disappointing; start with young plants in spring.

☼ ◊◊◊ ✽ 5-11   ❄ 5°C

SURFINIA *blue vein*
SOLANACEAE
See *S.* rose pink.

☼ ◊ ✽ 6-11   ❄ 5°C

☼ ◊◊◊ ✽ 5-11   ❄ 5°C

SURFINIA *purple vein*
SOLANACEAE
See *S.* rose pink.

SURFINIA *pink vein*
SOLANACEAE
See *S.* rose pink.

:☼: △△ ✿ 8-9   ❄ 5°C

SURALIA *pinnata*
Little is known about this plant.

:☼: △△ ✿ 7-9   ❄ 5°C

SYZYCHIUM *paniculatum*
MYRTACEAE
Splendid cultivar of the *myrte* family; fertilize moderately; needs acid soil and soft water; purple berries appear after flowering; keep rather dry at 5 °C in winter; could be trimmed in shape.

:☼: △△ ✿ 4-10   ❄ 0°C

TABERNAEMONTANA *divaricata*
BIGNONIACEAE
Propagation: by cuttings.
Fertilize regularly; fragrant; winter rather dry and frost-free.

:☼: △△△ ✿ 5-11   ❄ 5°C

TAGETES
ASTERACEAE/COMPOSITAE
Propagation: by seed.
Fertilize weekly; sow early spring; intolerant of excessive rainfall.

:☼: △△△ ✿ 5-11   ❄ 5°C

TAGETES *x patula*
ASTERACEAE/COMPOSITAE
See *Tagetes*.

:☼: △△△ ✿ 5-11   ❄ 5°C

TAGETES *x patula*
ASTERACEAE/COMPOSITAE
See *Tagetes*.

:☼: △△△ ✿ 5-11   ❄ 5°C

TAGETES 'Naughty Mariette'
ASTERACEAE/COMPOSITAE
See *Tagetes*.

:☼: △△△ ✿ 5-11   ❄ 5°C

TAGETES 'Striped Marvel'
ASTERACEAE/COMPOSITAE
See *Tagetes*.

:☼: △△△ ✿ 5-11   ❄ 5°C

TAGETES *x patula* yellow
ASTERACEAE/COMPOSITAE
See *Tagetes*.

☼ ◊◊ ✿ 8-10 ❄ -5°C

TECOMA ***capensis*** yellow
BIGNONIACEAE
Propagation: by cuttings.
Fertilize weekly; lovely, arching perennial; needs plenty of warmth to get flowers; cut hard back in autumn; keep rather dry and frost-free in winter; syn. *Tecomaria capensis*.

☼ ◊◊ ✿ 8-10 ❄ 5°C

TECOMA ***capensis*** orange
BIGNONIACEAE
Propagation: by cuttings.
Fertilize weekly; lovely, arching perennial; needs plenty of warmth to get flowers; cut hard back in autumn and keep rather dry and frost-free in winter; syn. *Tecomaria capensis*.

☼ ◊◊ ✿ 8-10 ❄ 5°C

TECOMA ***castanifolia***
BIGNONIACEAE
Propagation: by cuttings.
Fertilize weekly; large racemes of gold-yellow flowers; cut hard back in autumn; keep rather dry and frost-free in winter; syn. *T. gaudichaudi*.

☼ ◊◊ ✿ 7-10 ❄ 5°C

TECOMA ***x smithii***
BIGNONIACEAE
Propagation: by cuttings.
Fertilize weekly; large racemes of yellow flowers with an orange tinge; cut back in autumn; keep rather dry and frost-free in winter.

☼ ◊ ✿ 7-8 ❄ 12°C

THEVETIA ***peruviana***
APOCYNACEAE
Propagation: by cuttings.
Fertilize weekly; needs full sun, warmth and a sheltered place; splendid; prune sparingly; winter rather dry at 12 ºC.

☼ ◊ ✿ 7-8 ❄ 12°C

THEVETIA ***peruviana alba***
APOCYNACEAE
See *T. peruviana alba*.

☼ ◊ ✿ 7-8 ❄ 12°C

THEVETIA ***peruviana*** salmon
APOCYNACEAE
See *T. peruviana alba*.

☼ ◊◊ ✿ 6-7 ❄ -20°C

THYMUS ***citriodorus*** 'Aureus'
LABIATAE/LAMIACEAE
Propagation: by division.
Clump-forming perennial; culinary use; fragrant; produces a lilac-pink "cushion" in pots; dislikes overwatering; protect from excessive rainfall.

☼ ◊◊ ✿ 6-7 ❄ -20°C

THYMUS ***vulgaris compactus***
LABIATAE/LAMIACEAE
Propagation: by cuttings or division.
Clump-forming perennial; culinary use; fragrant; produces a lilac-pink "cushion" in pots; dislikes overwatering; protect from excessive rainfall.

☼ ◊◊◊ �֍ 6-10 ❄ 10°C

THUNBERGIA *alata* pale yellow
Annual climber; named 'Black-eyed Susan'.

☼ ◊◊◊ ✳ 6-10 ❄ 10°C

THUNBERGIA *alata* yellow

THUNBERGIA
ACANTHACEAE

Propagation: by cuttings.
Fertilize weekly; climbers and shrubs; trim climbers in autumn and keep rather dry at 10 °C in winter; *T. alata* will mostly been offered as annual, but could winter.

☼ ◊◊◊ ✳ 6-10 ❄ 10°C

THUNBERGIA bow
'Susan' trained along a bow.

☼ ◊◊◊ ✳ 6-10 ❄ 10°C

THUNBERGIA *alata* white

☼ ◊◊◊ ✳ 6-10 ❄ 10°C

THUNBERGIA *battiscombii*
Cobalt-blue flowers with yellow heart.

☼   ◊◊◊   ❀ 6-10   ❄ 10°C

THUNBERGIA *erecta*
Upright-growing shrub.

☼   ◊◊◊   ❀ 6-10   ❄ 10°C

THUNBERGIA *fragrans*
Fragrant, white flowers.

☼   ◊◊◊   ❀ 6-10   ❄ 10°C

THUNBERGIA *grandiflora*
Climber with soft blue flowers.

☼   ◊◊◊   ❀ 6-10   ❄ 10°C

THUNBERGIA *gregorii*
Often grown as annual, but is perennial.

☼   ◊◊◊   ❀ 6-10   ❄ 10°C

THUNBERGIA *gregorii x alata* yellow
A new hybrid – perennial.

☼   ◊◊◊   ❀ 6-10   ❄ 10°C

THUNBERGIA *lancifolia*
Large sky-blue flowers.

☼   ◊◊◊   ❀ 6-10   ❄ 10°C

THUNBERGIA *laurifolia*
Large cobalt-blue flowers.

☼   ◊◊◊   ❀ 6-10   ❄ 10°C

THUNBERGIA *mysorensis*
Evergreen climber; lovely along a pergola, resulting in splendid hanging flowers.

☼   ◊◊◊   ❀ 6-10   ❄ 10°C

THUNBERGIA *natalensis*
A blue *T. lancifolia*.

☀ ◊◊◊ ✿ 6-12 ❄ 6°C

TIBOUCHINA *gayana*
Creeping small shrub full of small white flowers;
lovely for baskets.

☀ ◊◊◊ ✿ 6-12 ❄ 6°C

TIBOUCHINA *grandiflora*
Splendid hairy leaves.

TIBOUCHINA
MELASTOMATACEAE

Propagation: by cuttings.
Fertilize weekly; cut older plants hard back in
autumn; keep rather dry at 6 ºC in winter; from
T. urvalliana (with splendid velvety-blue flowers,
but unfortunately rather late flowering) is an
improved cultivar on the market with the same
splendid flowers, but flowering much earlier;
there is also *T. nana* on the market; this plant
grows very compactly, flowers earlier and very
abundantly; year after year more species and cultivars appear, also in white and pink colours; all
worth growing.

☀ ◊◊◊ ✿ 6-12 ❄ 6°C

TIBOUCHINA hybrid improved form
Earlier flowering than *T. urvalliana*.

☀ ◊◊◊ ✿ 6-12 ❄ 6°C

TIBOUCHINA *melastoma*
Pretty pink flower.

☀ ◊◊◊ ✿ 6-12 ❄ 6°C

TIBOUCHINA *nana*
Mind the stamens.

☀ ◌◌◌ ✿ 6-12 ❄ 6°C

TIBOUCHINA *organensis*
Velvety-soft grey-green foliage.

☀ ◌◌◌ ✿ 6-12 ❄ 6°C

TIBOUCHINA *paratropica*
Creeping small shrub with pink flowers; for baskets.

☀ ◌◌◌ ✿ 67-12 ❄ 6°C

TIBOUCHINA *rosea*
Large pink flowers.

☀ ◌◌◌ ✿ 6-12 ❄ 6°C

TIBOUCHINA *viminalis*
Small shrub with violet flowers; rare.

☀ ◌◌◌ ✿ 6-12 ❄ 6°C

☀ ◌◌◌ ✿ 6-12 ❄ 6°C

TIBOUCHINA *viminalis*
Large plant.

TIBOUCHINA *urvalliana*
The well-known *tibouchina*.

☀ ◊◊◊ ❀ 6-9 ❄ 5°C

TORENIA *summerwave* 'Blue'
SCROPHULARIACEAE
Propagation: by seed.
Fertilize weekly; beautiful annual; suitable for pots and baskets.

☀ ◊◊ ❀ 4-11 ❄ 2°C

TRACHELOSPERMUM *jasminoides*
APOCYNACEAE
Propagation: by cuttings.
Fertilize weekly; evergreen climber; fragrant; resists some frost; trim long slender stems in autumn; keep rather dry and frost-free in winter.

☀ ◊◊ ❀ 6-9 ❄ 6°C

TROPAEOLUM double orange
TROPAEOLACEAE
Propagation: by seed.
Fertilize once a month; needs poor soil; splendid for pots and baskets.

☀ ◊◊ ❀ 6-10 ❄ 5°C

TROPAEOLUM *perigrinum*
TROPAEOLACEAE
Propagation: by seed.
Fertilize once a month; vigorous climber; lovely when trained along a wire-netting pillar; syn. *T. canariense.*

☀ ◊◊ ❀ 7-10 ❄ 5°C

TROPAEOLUM *tuberosum*
TROPAEOLACEAE
Propagation: by tubers.
Fertilize once a month; a perennial climber with tubers; keep rather dry and frost-free in winter.

☀ ◊◊ ❀ 6-9 ❄ 6°C

TROPAEOLUM double red
TROPAEOLACEAE
Propagation: by seed.
Fertilize once a month; needs poor soil; splendid for pots and baskets.

☀ ◊◊ ❀ 7-8 ❄ 5°C

TUMBELLINA 'Priscilla'
There is little known about this plant.

☀ ◊◊ ❀ 5-10 ❄ 5°C

TURNERIE *ulmifolia*
TURNERACEAE
Propagation: by cuttings.
Fertilize regularly; flowers are very short-living, but bloom over a long period; keep rather dry and frost-free in winter.

☀ ◊◊ ❀ 6-8 ❄ 10°C

UNCARINA *granderii*
PEDALIACEAE
Needs a sheltered place; water sparingly; keep dry in winter.

☀ ◊◊◊ ✽ 5-11 ❄ 4°C

VERBENA rose red

☀ ◊◊◊ ✽ 10-12 ❄ 4°C

VERBENA rose red with heart

VERBENA
VERBENACEAE

Propagation: by seed or cuttings.
Fertilize weekly; the last years have seen new forms from Japan, namely 'Tapien' and 'Pemari'; to prevent confusion in this book, only the name *Verbena* is used; there are trailing and upright-growing *verbenas*; both are floriferous and suitable for growing in pots and baskets; cut hard back in autumn and keep rather dry and frost-free during winter; it is better to make cuttings in autumn; winter these plants in a not too cold place and start each year with these new plants.

☀ ◊◊◊ ✽ 5-11 ❄ 4°C

VERBENA pale pink

☀ ◊◊◊ ✽ 5-11 ❄ 4°C

☀ ◊◊◊ ✽ 5-11 ❄ 4°C

VERBENA 'Peach and Cream'

VERBENA red with white heart

☀ ◊◊◊ ✿ 5-11   ❄ 4°C

VERBENA pale pink

☀ ◊◊◊ ✿ 5-11   ❄ 4°C

VERBENA red
Trailing.

☀ ◊ ✿ 5-11   ❄ 4°C

VERBENA rose
Small flowers.

☀ ◊◊◊ ✿ 5-11   ❄ 4°C

VERBENA lilac

☀ ◊◊◊ ✿ 5-11   ❄ 4°C

VERBENA pale pink

☀ ◊◊◊ ✿ 5-11   ❄ 4°C

VERBENA rose

☀ ◊◊◊ ✿ 5-11   ❄ 4°C

VERBENA purple
Trailing.

☀ ◊◊◊ ✿ 5-11   ❄ 4°C

VERBENA rose/light rose
Trailing.

☀ ◊◊◊ ✿ 5-11   ❄ 4°C

VERBENA rose-red
Trailing.

☼ ◊◊◊ ✿ 5-10 ❄ 3°C

VENEDIUM *fastuosum*
ASTERACEAE/COMPOSITAE
Propagation: by seed or cuttings.
Fertilize weekly; lovely when grown in pots; keep
rather dry in winter; it is better to start each year
with young plants; syn. *Arctotis fastuosum.*

☼ ◊◊◊ ✿ 5-10 ❄ 3°C

VENEDIUM
ASTERACEAE/COMPOSITAE
Propagation: by seed or cuttings.
Fertilize weekly; lovely when grown in pots; keep
rather dry in winter; it is better to start each year
with young plants; syn. *Arctotis fastuosum.*

☼ ◊◊ ✿ 6-7 ❄ -25°C

VERONICA *cantiana* 'Kentish Pink'
SCROPHULARIACEAE
Propagation: by division.
Fertilize regularly if grown in pots; sprouts roots
easy; pretty perennial with long slender stems
trailing over the baskets.

☼ ◊◊ ✿ 4-6 ❄ -25°C

VERONICA *peduncularis* 'George Blue'
Propagation: by division.
Fertilize regularly if grown in pots; early-flower-
ing; lovely perennial for pots and containers.

◐ ◊◊ ✿ 9-4 ❄ -8°C

VIBURNUM *tinus* 'Eve Price'
CAPRIFOLIACEAE
Propagation: by cuttings.
Fertilize regularly if grown in pots; protect from
severe frost; could be trimmed into shape; attrac-
tive because of its winter flowering.

◐ ◊◊ ✿ 9-4 ❄ -8°C

VIBURNUM *tinus* 'Gwellian'
CAPRIFOLIACEAE
Propagation: by cuttings.
Fertilize regularly if grown in pots; protect from
severe frost; can be trimmed into shape; attractive
because of its winter flowering; dark-rose buds.

☼ ◊◊ ✿ 6-7 ❄ 5°C

WASHINGTONIA *robusta*
ARECACEAE/PALMAE
Fertilize regularly; needs well-drained soil; keep
rather dry and frost-free in winter.

☼ ◊◊ ✿ 5-7 ❄ 2°C

WATTAKAKA *sinensis*
ASCLEPIADACEAE
Propagation: by cuttings.
Fertilize weekly; fragrant climber; trimming is not
a necessity, but an overly large plant could be cut
back in autumn; keep rather dry and frost-free in
winter.

☼ ◊◊ ✿ 4-9 ❄ 5°C

WESTRINGIA *fruticosa*
LABIATAE/LAMIACEAE
Propagation: by cuttings.
Fertilize regularly; a rather unknown shrub; trim
in autumn and keep rather dry at 5 °C in winter.

☀ ◌◌◌ ✿ 5-9   ❄ -15°C

VIOLA 'Winona Cawthorne'
VIOLACEAE
Propagation: by cuttings in autumn.
Fertilize regularly; winter rather dry or start next
year with young plants.

☀ ◌◌◌ ✿ 5-9   ❄ -15°C

VIOLA 'Columbine'
VIOLACEAE
See *V.* 'Winona Cawthorne'.

☀ ◌◌ ✿ 3-5   ❄ -25°C

VIOLA *odorata*
VIOLACEAE
See *V.* 'Winona Cawthorne'.

☀ ◌◌◌ ✿ 4-6   ❄ 5°C

VIOLA hybrid
VIOLACEAE
See *V.* 'Winona Cawthorne'.

☀ ◌◌ ✿ 3-5   ❄ -15°C

VIOLA *x wittrockiana*
VIOLACEAE
Propagation: by cuttings.
Fertilize regularly if grown in pots; because of its
early flowers, suitable for pots on a terrace.

☀ ◌◌ ✿ 4-5   ❄ 5°C

VIOLA hybrid
VIOLACEAE
Propagation: by cuttings.
Fertilize regularly if grown in pots; cheers up a
terrace in spring.

List of common names

African Blue Lily . . . . *Agapanthus umbellatus*
African Hemp . . . . *Sparmannia africana*
Angels' Trumpets . . . . *Brugmansia*
Arabicus . . . . *Ophiopogon planiscapus Nigrescens*
Balsam . . . . *Impatiens*
Bay laurel . . . . *Laurus nobilis*
Black dragon . . . . *Ophiopogon planiscapus Nigrescens*
Blood flower . . . . *Asclepias currasavica*
Blue glory bower . . . . *Clerodendron ugandese*
Blue Hibiscus . . . . *Alyogyne hueglii*
Bottlebrush . . . . *Callistemon*
Busy Lizzie . . . . *Impatiens*
Calamint . . . . *Calamintha*
Canary Island date palm . . . . *Phoenix canariensis*
Carnation . . . . *Dianthus*
Castor oil plant . . . . *Ricinus communis*
Cat's Paw . . . . *Anigozanthos*
Cherry pie . . . . *Heliotropium arborescens*
Chilli pepper . . . . *Albizzia julibrissin*
Christmas Rose . . . . *Helleborus niger*
Cigar flower . . . . *Cuphea ignea*
Cock's comb . . . . *Erythrina crista-galli*
Common coral tree . . . . *Erythrina crista-galli*
Coral flower . . . . *Heuchera*
Coral gem . . . . *Lotus berthelotii*
Crane flower . . . . *Strelitzia reginae*
Creeping blueblossom . . . . . *Ceanothus thyrsoflorus var. repens*
Cruel plant . . . . *Araujia sericofera*
Daisy . . . . *Bellis*
Dusty miller . . . . *Lychnis coronaria*
Ebony knight . . . . *Ophiopogon planiscapus Nigrescens*
Elephant-eared saxifrage . . . . *Bergenia*
Elephant's ears . . . . *Bergenia*
Fleabane . . . . *Erigeron karvinskianus*
Fritillary . . . . *Fritillaria*
Garland lily . . . . *Hedychium*
Ginger lily . . . . *Hedychium*
Glory of the snow . . . . *Chionodoxa*
Golden creeping Jenny . . . . *Lysimachia nummularia*
Granadilla . . . . *Passiflora*
Heliotrope . . . . *Heliotropium arborescens*
Helmet flower . . . . *Scutellaria*
Indian root . . . . *Asclepias currasavica*
Ivy . . . . *Hedera*
Japanese Sago Palm . . . . *Cycas revoluta*
Kangaroo Paw . . . . *Anigozanthos*
Lavender . . . . *Lavandula*
Leadwort . . . . *Plumbago*
Lemon Verbena . . . . *Aloysia citrodora*
Lion's ear . . . . *Leonotis leonuris*
Loquat . . . . *Eriobotrya japonica*
Lungwort . . . . *Pulmonaria*
Marigold . . . . *Tagetes*
Marjoram . . . . *Origanum*
Mezereon . . . . *Daphne mesereum*
Mint . . . . *Mentha*
Monkey flower . . . . *Mimulus*

Musk . . . . *Mimulus*
Navelwort . . . . *Omphalodes cappadocica*
Oleander . . . . *Nerium oleander*
Olive . . . . *Olea europaea*
Oregano . . . . *Origanum*
Pansy . . . . *Viola*
Paprika . . . . *Capsicum annuum*
Parrot's beak . . . . *Lotus berthelotii*
Passion flower . . . . *Passiflora*
Pelican's beak . . . . *Lotus berthelotii*
Pineapple flower . . . . *Eucomis*
Pineapple lily . . . . *Eucomis*
Pink . . . . *Dianthus*
Plantain Lily . . . . *Hosta*
Pohutakawa . . . . *Metrosideros*
Pomegranate . . . . *Punica*
Pride of Madeira . . . . *Echium fastuosum*
Primrose . . . . *Primula*
Rata . . . . *Metrosideros*
Rattlebox . . . . *Crotularia*
Red ginger . . . . *Alpinia purpurata*
Rock cress . . . . *Arabis*
Rock rose . . . . *Cistus*
Rose campion . . . . *Lychnis coronaria*
Rosemary . . . . *Rosmarinus*
Sage . . . . *Salvia*
Sea Pink . . . . *Armeria juniperifolia*
Shamrock . . . . *Oxalis*
Silk tree . . . . *Albizzia julibrissin*
Skullcap . . . . *Scutellaria*
Snapdragon . . . . *Antirrhynum*
Snowdrop . . . . *Galanthus*
Sorrel . . . . *Oxalis, Veronica cantiana*
Speedwell . . . . *Veronica peduncularis*
Spider Flower . . . . *Cleome*
Stonecrop . . . . *Sedum*
Strawberry tree . . . . *Arbutus unedo*
Sun rose . . . . *Cistus*
Swallow-wort . . . . *Asclepias currasavica*
Sweet laurel . . . . *Laurus nobilis*
Sweet William . . . . *Dianthus barbatus*
Thyme . . . . *Thymus*
Tobacco plant . . . . *Nicotiana*
Trailing Abutilon . . . . *Abutilon megapotamica*
Tree Tomato . . . . *Cyphomandra betacea*
Variegated ground ivy . . . . *Glechoma hederacea var.*
Violet . . . . *Viola*
Wallflower . . . . *Erysimum*
Wattle . . . . *Acacia*
Yesterday, today, and tomorrow . . . . *Brunfelsia pauciflora*

Indices

HANGING PLANTS

Anagallis monelli
Anagallis 'Scarlet'
Antirrhynum lilac
Antirrhynum yellow and white
Bacopa 'Snowflake'
Begonia sutherlandii
Bidens ferulifolia aurea
Bougainvillea glabra
Bougainvillea glabra light
Bougainvillea 'Rosenka'
Bougainvillea 'Australian Gold'
Bowiea volubilis
Brachyscome
Brachyscome iberifolia
Centradenia
Clematis cartmanii 'Joe'
Clematis forsteri
Coleus 'Meltencave' or 'Aubergine Jewel'
Convolvulus mauritanicus
Diascia
Epilobium glauca
Erigeron karvinskianus
Erysimum 'Moonlight'
Fuchsia procumbens
Glechoma hederacea variegata
Isotoma axillaris
Lantana montevidensis lavender
Lantana montevidensis pink
Lantana montevidensis white
Lobelia erinus 'Cambridge Blue'
Lotus berthelotii
Lotus berthelotii 'Gold'
Lotus jacobeus
Lotus nigrescens
Lysimachia nummularia
Manettia inflata
'Million Bells' red
'Million Bells' yellow
'Million Bells' Cherry
'Million Bells' white
'Million Bells' Carillon Blue
Mimulus aurantiacus white
Mimulus bifidus 'Wine'
Mimulus glutinosus 'Monkey Musk'
Mimulus 'Strawberry Wine'
Mimulus 'Tangerine'
Mimulus white *x aurantiacus*
Nemesia strumosa 'KLM'
Nemesia strumosa 'Mello Red and White'
Nemesia strumosa 'Mello White'
Nolana paradoxa
Oxalis
Oxalis bowiei
Oxalis hirta
Oxalis lobata
Oxalis obtusa
Passiflora citrina
Passiflora karwinski
Passiflora sanguinolenta
Pelargonium decora red

Pelargonium 'Ville de Paris'
Pelargonium 'L'elegante'
Petunia
Russelia equisetiformis alba
Russelia equisetiformis
Sanvitalia
Scaevola aemula 'Blue Fan'
Scaevola aemula 'Alba'
Scutellaria costaricana
Sphaeralcea munroana compacta
Streptocarpus saxorum
Surfinias
Tibouchina gayana
Tibouchina paratropica
Torenia 'Summerwave Blue'
Tropaeolum
Verbena
Veronica cantiana 'Kentish Pink'

CLIMBING PLANTS

Allamanda carthartica
Allamanda carthartica 'Cherry Sunset'
Allamanda carthartica 'Chocolate Swirl'
Allamanda carthartica hendersonii
Allamanda schottii
Allamanda violacea
Angelonia rosea
Angelonia gardneri
Araujia sericofera
Aristolochia fimbriata
Asarina barclayana
Asarina scandens 'Bride's White'
Beaumontia grandiflora
Campsis grandiflora
Campsis radicans 'Flamingo'
Campsis radicans flava
Clerodendron thomsoniae
Clerodendron ugandese
Clitorea ternata
Cobaea scandens
Glechoma hederacea variegata
Hardenbergia violacea alba
Hardenbergia violacea
Hardenbergia violacea 'Pink Cascade'
Hibbertia scandens
Ipomoea alba
Ipomoea indica
Ipomoea leari
Ipomoea mauritiana
Ipomoea purpurea
Jasminum angulare
Jasminum azoricum
Jasminum mesnyi
Jasminum officinale
Jasminum polyanthum
Kennedia coccinea
Kennedia nigricans
Lapageria rosea
Mandevilla 'Alice du Pont'
Mandevilla amabilis

Mandevilla boliviensis
Mandevilla sanderi rosea
Mandevilla sanderi 'Scarlet Pimpernel'
Mandevilla suaveolens
Manettia inflata
Mimulus aurantiacus white
Mimulus bifidus 'Wine'
Mimulus glutinosus 'Monkey Musk'
Mimulus 'Strawberry Wine'
Mimulus 'Tangerine'
Mimulus white x aurantiacus
Monopsis kapablue
Pandorea jasminoides
Pandorea jasminoides 'Alba'
Pandorea jasminoides 'Rosea'
Passiflora x arisa
Passiflora auranticum
Passiflora caerulea
Passiflora caerulea x amethystina
Passiflora caerulea x racemosa
Passiflora cincinnata
Passiflora edulis 'Knight'
Passiflora 'Elizabeth'
Passiflora x exoniensis
Passiflora herbertiana
Passiflora incarnata
Passiflora incarnata alba
Passiflora 'Kaiserin Eugénie'
Passiflora 'Lavender Lady'
Passiflora mixta
Passiflora morifolia
Passiflora naviculata
Passiflora peresii
Passiflora 'Sunburst'
Passiflora vitifolia
Pereskia corrilata
Pereskia grandiflora
Pereskia sacharosa
Phasaeolus caracalla
Plumbago auriculata
Plumbago auriculata alba
Podranea brysei
Podranea ricasoliana
Quamoclit pennata
Quamoclit pennata orange
Rhodochiton atrosanguineus
Senecio confusus large
Senecio confusus small
Solandra maxima
Solanum aviculare
Solanum bonariense
Solanum crispum 'Glasnevin'
Solanum jasminoides
Solanum muricatum
Solanum quioense
Solanum rantonnettii
Solanum rantonnettii 'Outre Mer'
Solanum rantonnettii 'Royal Robe'
Thunbergia alata light yellow
Thunbergia alata white
Thunbergia battiscombii
Thunbergia grandiflora
Thunbergia gregorii
Thunbergia gregorii x alata yellow
Thunbergia lancifolia
Thunbergia laurifolia

Thunbergia natalensis
Trachelospermum jasminoides
Tropaeolum
Tropaeolum perigrinum
Tropaeolum tuberosum
Wattakaka sinensis

BERRY- OR FRUIT-BEARING

Acca sellowiana
Arbutus unedo
Asclepias fruticosa
Asclepias physocarpus
Capparis frondosa
Capsicum annuum
Carissa grandiflora
Carissa macrocarpa
Carissa nana
Citrus
Coffea arabica
Cyphomandra betacea
Daphne mesereum 'Rubra'
Duranta repens
Duranta repens alba
Eriobotrya japonica
Ficus carica
Fuchsia arborescens
Grevillea rosmarinifolia
Hedera helix arborescens
Lagunaria patersonii
Murraya exotica
Musa violacea
Olea europaea
Passiflora caerulea
Passiflora x exoniensis
Passiflora herbertiana
Passiflora morifolia
Pernettya mucronata 'Lilacina'
Pernettya mucronata 'Alba'
Phoenix canariensis
Psidium guajave
Punica granatum
Punica granatum flora plena
Skimmia laureola 'Kew White'
Skimmia reevesiana
Solanum aviculare
Solanum muricatum
Solanum quioense

BLOOMING IN EARLY SPRING

Acacia 'Claire de Lune'
Acacia retinodes 'Lise'
Acacia 'St. Helena'
Acacia 'Tournaire'
Anemone blanda
Anemone blanda 'White Splendour'
Azalea
Bergenia 'Silberlicht'
Bergenia 'Admiraal'
Camellia
Cardamine quinquefolia
Ceanothus thyrsiflorus var. repens
Chamaelaucium uncinatum

Chionodoxa luciliae
Clematis cartmanii 'Joe'
Clerodendron wallichii
Correa 'Mannii'
Crocus tommasinianus 'Barr's Purple'
Crocus tommasinianus
Crocus 'Zwanenburg Brons'
Daphne mesereum 'Rubra'
Diosma hirsutum 'Pink Fountain'
Eranthemum nervosum
Fremontodendron californicum
Fritillaria imperialis lutea
Fritillaria imperialis rubra
Fritillaria persica
Galanthus nivalis
Grevillea juniperina
Grevillea longifolia
Grevillea 'Mount Tamboritha'
Grevillea rosmarinifolia
Kennedia nigricans
Mahonia japonica
Narcissus cyclamineus 'Tête à Tête'
Narcissus odorus plenus
Omphalodes cappadocica 'Starry Eyes'
Parahebe catarractae
Primula x pubescens
Primula vulgaris 'Double White'
Primula vulgaris subsp. sibthorpii
Pulmonaria saccharata
Reinwardtia indica
Rhododendron praecox
Veronica peduncularis 'George Blue'
Viola x wittrockiana

ATTRACTIVE IN WINTER

Buxus
Helleborus niger
Heuchera 'Rachel'
Heuchera 'Stormy Seas'
Leucothoe axillaris
Leucothoe walterii 'Rainbow'
Ophiopogon planiscapus Nigrescens
Pernettya mucronata 'Lilacina'
Pernettya mucronata 'Alba'
Sarcococca confusa
Sarcococca ruscifolia
Skimmia laureola 'Kew White'
Skimmia reevesiana
Skimmia japonica rubella
Viburnum tinus 'Eve Price'
Viburnum tinus 'Gwellian'

GOOD-LOOKING FOLIAGE

Agave americana
Agave americana marginata aurea
Aloe arborescens
Aloe 'Campert Schweinfurth'
Asystasia gangetica alba
Chamaecyparis lawsoniana 'Nana'
Chamaerops humilis
Chrysalidocarpus lutescens
Coleus 'Brisana'

Coleus 'Meltencave' or 'Aubergine Jewel'
Coleus 'Morgenlava'
Coleus 'Ottoman'
Coleus 'Pineapple Beauty'
Cordaline australis
Cycas revoluta
Dracaena marginata
Echium fastuosum
Glechoma hederacea variegata
Hebe andersonii variegata
Hebe canterburiensis
Hebe diosmifolia
Hedera helix arborescens
Helichrysum petiolare
Helichrysum petiolare gold
Helichrysum petiolare silver
Helichrysum microphyllum
Hosta 'Blue Cadet'
Hosta fortunei 'Patriot'
Hosta sieboldii 'Snowflake'
Hosta 'Wide Brim'
Laurus nobilis
Lavatera 'Barnsley'
Leucothoe axillaris
Leucothoe walterii 'Rainbow'
Myrtus communis
Myrtus communis nana
Ophiopogon planiscapus Nigrescens
Pelargonium 'Hills of Snow'
Pelargonium 'L'elegante'
Pelargonium 'Robert Fish'
Phoenix canariensis
Washingtonia robusta

ODORIFEROUS PLANTS

Aloysia citrodora
Angelonia alba
Angelonia rosea
Beaumontia grandiflora
Bidens ferulifolia aurea
Bouvardia longiflora
Brugmansia arb. 'Engels Glocken'
Brugmansia aurea x arborescens
Brugmansia candida 'Cinderella'
Brugmansia candida 'Double White'
Brugmansia candida 'Weisz'
Brugmansia 'Gelber Riese'
Brugmansia suaveolens 'Gold'
Brugmansia suaveolens 'Goldtraum'
Brugmansia versicolor
Brugmansia versicolor 'Kew'
Brugmansia sanguinea flava
Brugmansia candida plena
Brunfelsia hopeana
Calamintha nepeta subsp. Nepeta
Carissa grandiflora
Carissa macrocarpa
Carissa nana
Cestrum nocturnum
Chamaelaucium uncinatum
Choisya 'Aztec Pride'
Choisya ternata
Citrus
Clerodendron bungei

Clerodendron fragrans
Cobaea scandens
Crinum powelli
Daphne mesereum 'Rubra'
Dianthus
Dianthus barbatus
Dombeya wallichii
Eriobotrya japonica
Eucalyptus radiata
Gardenia jasminoides
Gardenia augusta 'August B.'
Gardenia 'Belmone'
Gardenia 'Coral Gold'
Gardenia 'Miami Supreme'
Heliotropium amplexicaule
Heliotropium arborescens
Heliotropium arborescens alba
Heliotropium alba
Jasminum angulare
Jasminum azoricum
Jasminum nitidum
Jasminum officinale
Jasminum polyanthum
Jasminum revolutum
Jasminum sambac
Lavandula angustifolia alba
Lavandula dentata
Lavandula stoechas
Leucaena leucocephala
Ligustrum japonicum texanum
Mentha
Mentha longifolia 'Buddleia'
Murraya exotica
Narcissus odorus plenus
Nicotiana glauca
Nicotiana alata
Origanum 'Bristol Cross'
Origanum 'Pagoda Bells'
Passiflora cincinnata
Passiflora karwinski
Passiflora 'Kaiserin Eugénie'
Prostanthera cuneata
Psidium guajave
Rosmarinus officinalis 'Boule'
Salvias
Senecio heritieri
Tabernaemontana divaricata
Thunbergia fragrans
Thymus citriodorus 'Aureus'
Thymus vulgaris compactus
Viola odorata
Wattakaka sinensis

ANNUALS

Alyssum 'Snow Crystals'
Anagallis monelli
Anagallis 'Scarlet'
Antirrhynum purple pink
Antirrhynum white and yellow
Bacopa 'Snowflake'
Bellis perennis
Brachyscome iberifolia
Brachyscome
Brachyscome iberifolia

Brassica
Capsicum annuum
Celosia
Celosia argentea pyramidalis
Cleome spinosa 'Cherry Queen'
Cleome spinosa 'Helen Campbell'
Cleome dark pink
Dianthus barbatus
Dimorphoteca aurea
Felicia ameloides blue
Felicia ameloides variegata
Felicia ameloides variegata alba
Gazania
Impatiens
Isotoma axillaris
Limnanthus douglasii
Lobelia erinus 'Cambridge Blue'
'Million Bells' red
'Million Bells' yellow
'Million Bells' Cherry
'Million Bells' white
'Million Bells' Carillon Blue
Nemesia strumosa 'KLM'
Nemesia strumosa 'Mello Red and White'
Nemesia strumosa 'Mello White'
Nicotiana alata
Nolana paradoxa
Osteospermum
Petunia
Portulaca
Quamoclit pennata
Quamoclit pennata orange
Ranunculus
Rosmarinus officinalis 'Sissinghurst White'
Salvia splendens violet
Salvia splendens red
Salvia splendens pink
Sanvitalia
Surfinias
Tagetes
Thunbergia alata light yellow
Thunbergia alata white
Torenia 'Summerwave Blue'
Tropaeolum perigrinum
Venedium fastuosum
Verbena
Viola x wittrockiana

PLANTS ATTRACTING BEES AND BUTTERFLIES

Asclepias currasavica
Asclepias currasavica 'Silky Gold'
Asclepias fruticosa
Asclepias physocarpus
Limnanthus douglasii
Linaria purpurea
Lobelia erinus 'Cambridge Blue'
Mentha
Mentha longifolia 'Buddleia'
Origanum 'Bristol Cross'
Origanum 'Pagoda Bells'
Rosmarinus officinalis 'Boule'
Rosmarinus officinalis 'Sissinghurst White'

Thymus citriodorus 'Aureus'
Thymus vulgaris compactus

GOOD-LOOKING SOLITARIES

Abutilon 'Boule de Neige'
Abutilon 'Citronella'
Abutilon 'Lemon Bells'
Abutilon 'Mini Orange'
Abutilon 'Orange Vein'
Abutilon 'Yellow Bells'
Abutilon 'Souvenir de Bonn'
Abutilon 'Giant Yellow'
Agapanthus umbellatus
Agapanthus umbellatus alba
Agapanthus 'Blue Giant'
Agapanthus 'Blue Moon'
Agave americana
Agave americana marginata aurea
Allamanda carthartica
Allamanda carthartica 'Cherry Sunset'
Allamanda carthartica 'Chocolate Swirl'
Allamanda carthartica hendersonii
Allamanda schottii
Allamanda violacea
Asclepias currasavica
Asclepias currasavica 'Silky Gold'
Asclepias fruticosa
Asclepias physocarpus
Bauhinia tomentosa
Begonia
Bougainvillea 'Appleblossom'
Bougainvillea 'California Gold'
Bougainvillea 'Italia Pink'
Bougainvillea spectabilis
Bouvardia longiflora
Brugmansia arb. 'Engels Glocken'
Brugmansia aurea x arborescens
Brugmansia candida 'Cinderella'
Brugmansia candida 'Double White'
Brugmansia candida 'Weisz'
Brugmansia 'Gelber Riese'
Brugmansia suaveolens 'Gold'
Brugmansia suaveolens 'Goldtraum'
Brugmansia versicolor
Brugmansia versicolor 'Kew'
Brugmansia sanguinea flava
Brugmansia candida plena
Brunfelsia hopeana
Brunfelsia pauciflora
Brunfelsia pauciflora 'Macrantha'
Canna indica red
Cassia artemisioides
Cassia corymbosa
Cassia didymobotria
Cassia floribunda
Clerodendron bungei
Clerodendron ugandese
Curcuma alisilatifolia
Erythrina x bidwillii
Erythrina crista-galli
Erythrina fespatidia
Erythrina herbacea
Eucomis bicolor
Fremontodendron californicum

Fuchsia arborescens
Fuchsia cordifolia
Fuchsia fulgens rubra grandiflora
Fuchsia juntasensis
Hedychium coronarium
Hedychium gardnerianum
Hibiscus acetosella
Hibiscus 'Double Mini Skirt'
Hibiscus 'Charles September'
Hibiscus 'Geisha'
Hibiscus 'Janys'
Hibiscus 'Jim Hendry'
Hibiscus 'Mystic Pink'
Hibiscus coccineus
Hibiscus moscheutos
Hibiscus mutabilis
Hibiscus trionum
Hibiscus schizopetalus
Iochroma cyaneum
Iochroma grandiflora light variety
Iochroma purpureum
Iochroma warscewiczii
Ipomoea alba
Ipomoea fistulosa
Ipomoea leari
Ipomoea mauritiana
Ipomoea purpurea
Isoplexis isabelliana
Isoplexis canariensis
Jasminum angulare
Jasminum azoricum
Jasminum nitidum
Jasminum officinale
Jasminum polyanthum
Jasminum revolutum
Lagunaria patersonii
Lantana sellowiana alba
Lantana camara 'Butterfly'
Lantana camara 'Cupfer Riese'
Lantana camara 'Goldsonne'
Lantana camara 'Ingelsheimer'
Lantana camara 'Old Rose'
Lantana camara 'Slot Ortenburg'
Lavatera maritima
Leptospermum scoparium light pink double
Leptospermum scoparium 'Red Dam'
Leptospermum scoparium pink
Leptospermum scoparium dark blue
Mandevilla 'Alice du Pont'
Mandevilla amabilis
Mandevilla boliviensis
Mandevilla sanderi rosea
Mandevilla sanderi 'Scarlet Pimpernel'
Mandevilla suaveolens
Nerium oleander 'Album'
Nerium oleander 'Alassio'
Nerium oleander 'Alsace'
Nerium oleander 'Luteum Pplenum'
Nerium oleander 'Mont Blanc'
Nerium oleander 'Petite Red'
Nerium oleander 'Petite Salmon'
Nerium oleander 'Sealy Pink'
Nerium oleander 'Soleil Levant'
Nerium oleander 'Ville de la Londe'
Pandorea jasminoides

Pandorea jasminoides 'Alba'
Pandorea jasminoides 'Rosea'
Podranea brysei
Podranea ricasoliana
Solanum bonariense
Solanum crispum 'Glasnevin'
Solanum jasminoides
Solanum rantonnettii
Solanum wendlandii
Tibouchina nana
Tibouchina urvalliana
Wattakaka sinensis

RECOMMENDED YELLOWS

Abutilon 'Citronella'
Abutilon 'Lemon Bells'
Abutilon 'Yellow Bells'
Abutilon 'Giant Yellow'
Allamanda carthartica
Arctotheca
Asclepias currasavica 'Silky Gold'
Bauhinia tomentosa
Bidens ferulifolia aurea
Bougainvillea 'California Gold'
Bougainvillea 'Australian Gold'
Brugmansia 'Gelber Riese'
Brugmansia suaveolens 'Gold'
Brugmansia suaveolens 'Goldtraum'
Brugmansia sanguinea flava
Cassia artemisioides
Cassia corymbosa
Cassia didymobotria
Cassia floribunda
Cestrum hybrid apricot-coloured
Cestrum nocturnum
Crotularia agatiflora
Cytisus 'Porlock'
Cytisus x racemosa
Erysimum 'Moonlight'
Fremontodendron californicum
Jasminum 'Mesnyi'
Jasminum revolutum
Juanulla aurantiaca
Lantana camara 'Cupfer Riese'
Lantana camara 'Goldsonne'
Lantana camara 'Ingelsheimer'
Lantana yellow
Limnanthus douglasii
Lysimachia nummularia
Medicago arborea
'Million Bells' yellow
Mussaendra 'Snowflake'
Nerium oleander 'Luteum Plenum'
Phygelius aqualis 'Yellow Trumpet'
Reinwardtia indica
Streptosolen jamesonii yellow
Tagetes
Tecoma capensis yellow
Tecoma castanifolia
Tecoma x smithii
Thevetia peruviana
Thunbergia alata light yellow
Thunbergia gregorii
Thunbergia gregorii x alata yellow

RECOMMENDED ORANGES

Abutilon 'Mini Orange'
Abutilon 'Orange Vein'
Abutilon 'Souvenir de Bonn'
Asclepias currasavica
Bougainvillea 'California Gold'
Bougainvillea 'Rosenka'
Cestrum aurantiacum
Lantana camara 'Butterfly'
Lantana camara 'Slot Ortenburg'
Lantana orange
Leonotis leonuris
Mimulus 'Tangerine'
Punica granatum
Punica granatum flora plena
Quamoclit pennata orange
Senecio confusus large
Senecio confusus small
Streptosolen jamesonii orange
Tagetes
Tecoma capensis orange
Tropaeolum

RECOMMENDED REDS

Alpinia purpurata
Anagallis 'Scarlet'
Cestrum newellii
Cytisus canariensis
Dahlia 'Bishop of Llandaff'
Hibiscus 'Double Mini Skirt'
Hibiscus 'Geisha'
Hibiscus coccineus
Hibiscus moscheutos
Jatropha integerrima
Jatropha podagrica
Kennedia coccinea
Leptospermum scoparium 'Red Dam'
Mandevilla sanderi 'Scarlet Pimpernel'
'Million Bells' red
'Million Bells' Cherry
Mimulus bifidus 'Wine'
Mimulus 'Strawberry Wine'
Nemesia strumosa 'Mello Red and White'
Nerium oleander 'Alassio'
Nerium oleander 'Alsace'
Nerium oleander 'Petite Red'
Nerium oleander 'Ville de la Londe'
Pentas lanceolata 'Royal Red'
Quamoclit pennata
Russelia equisetiformis
Salvia splendens red
Tropaeolum
Verbena

RECOMMENDED PINKS

Allamanda carthartica 'Cherry Sunset'
Angelonia rosea
Bougainvillea var. 'Dwarf Pink'
Bougainvillea 'Italia Pink'
Bougainvillea spectabilis
Fuchsia arborescens

Hardenbergia violacea 'Pink Cascade'
Hibiscus schizopetalus
Ipomoea fistulosa
Lantana camara 'Ingelsheimer'
Lantana camara 'Old Rose'
Lantana montevidensis pink
Lavatera 'Barnsley'
Leptospermum scoparium light pink double
Leptospermum scoparium pink
Mandevilla 'Alice du Pont'
Mandevilla amabilis
Mandevilla sanderi rosea
Medinella magnifica
Nerium oleander 'Sealy Pink'
Pandorea jasminoides
Pandorea jasminoides 'Rosea'
Pentas lanceolata 'Paradise'
Pentas lanceolata 'Bright Pink'
Pentas lanceolata 'Pink'
Pentas lanceolata 'Candy Stripe'
Salvia splendens pink
Tibouchina melastoma
Tibouchina rosea
Verbena

RECOMMENDED WHITES

Acnictus australis alba
Agapanthus umbellatus alba
Alyssum 'Snow Crystals'
Angelonia alba
Anthemis punctata subsp. cupaniana
Antirrhynum white and yellow
Arabis flora plena
Asarina scandens 'Bride's White'
Bacopa 'Snowflake'
Bougainvillea 'Appleblossom'
Bouvardia longiflora
Brugmansia arb. 'Engels Glocken'
Brugmansia candida 'Double White'
Brugmansia candida 'Weisz'
Brugmansia versicolor
Brugmansia versicolor 'Kew'
Brugmansia candida plena
Carpenteria californica
Choisya 'Aztec Pride'
Choisya ternata
Cistus cyprius
Cistus salviifolius
Citrus
Convolvulus cneorum
Duranta repens alba
Felicia ameloides variegata alba
Gardenia jasminoides
Gardenia augusta 'August B.'
Gardenia 'Belmone'
Gardenia 'Coral Gold'
Gardenia 'Miami Supreme'
Hardenbergia violacea alba
Heliotropium arborescens alba
Heliotropium alba
Hosta sieboldii 'Snowflake'
Ipomoea alba
Jasminum angulare

Jasminum azoricum
Jasminum nitidum
Jasminum officinale
Jasminum polyanthum
Jasminum sambac
Lantana sellowiana alba
Lantana montevidensis white
Ligustrum japonicum texanum
Limnanthus douglasii
Mandevilla boliviensis
'Million Bells' white
Mimulus aurantiacus white
Murraya exotica
Mussaendra 'Snowflake'
Myrtus communis
Myrtus communis nana
Nemesia strumosa 'Mello White'
Nerium oleander 'Album'
Nerium oleander 'Mont Blanc'
Pandorea jasminoides 'Alba'
Pelargonium stellar 'Arctic Star'
Pentas lanceolata 'Alba'
Plumbago auriculata alba
Rosmarinus officinalis 'Sissinghurst White'
Russelia equisetiformis alba
Scaevola aemula 'Alba'
Solanum bonariense
Solanum jasminoides
Thevetia peruviana alba
Thunbergia alata white
Verbena
Wattakaka sinensis

RECOMMENDED BLUES

Acnictus australis
Agapanthus umbellatus
Agapanthus 'Blue Giant'
Agapanthus 'Blue Moon'
Alyogyne hueglii
Anagallis monelli
Angelonia gardneri
Brachyscome iberifolia
Brachyscome
Brachyscome iberifolia
Brunfelsia hopeana
Brunfelsia pauciflora
Brunfelsia pauciflora 'Macrantha'
Clerodendron ugandese
Convolvulus mauretanicum
Duranta repens
Eranthemum nervosum
Felicia ameloides blue
Felicia ameloides variegata
Hardenbergia violacea
Heliotropium arborescens
Iochroma cyaneum
Iochroma grandiflora
Iochroma purpureum
Iochroma warscewiczii
Ipomoea leari
Ipomoea purpurea
Lobelia erinus 'Cambridge Blue'
'Million Bells' Carillon Blue